WHAT SMALL GROUP L
MEMBERS ARE SAYING
EXPERIENCING CHRIST TOG

D0199473

My group was formed four years ago of very new believers. EXPERIENCING CHRIST TOGETHER has helped form bonds, and we have fallen in love with Christ. We have had many trials, but we have learned to lean on the body of Christ to carry us through the difficult times. I know our lives are richer than ever.

—Leader

The EXPERIENCING CHRIST TOGETHER series has motivated me more than any other Bible study that I have ever been to. This Bible study gets to the heart of the matter—my character in Christ—and that has created action on my part.

—Leader

I love the fact that Jesus' life shows us how to live.

—Member

This series is an "awakening." Jesus has become a very personal friend.

—Leader

This series is definitely a must-do as the foundation for a healthy, maturing small group!

—Leader

EXPERIENCING CHRIST TOGETHER is a safe place to learn about the living Jesus and how he wants to lead us and love us.

—Member

EXPERIENCING CHRIST TOGETHER ties the heart and the mind together. The Bible knowledge grows the mind and the life application grows the heart and transforms the soul.

—Member

Other Studies in the EXPERIENCING CHRIST TOGETHER Series

Beginning in Christ Together (Life of Jesus)

Connecting in Christ Together (Fellowship)

Growing in Christ Together (Discipleship)

Serving Like Christ Together (Ministry)

Surrendering to Christ Together (Worship)

Studies in the DOING LIFE TOGETHER Series

Beginning Life Together (God's Purpose for Your Life)

Connecting with God's Family (Fellowship)

Growing to Be Like Christ (Discipleship)

Developing Your SHAPE to Serve Others (Ministry)

Sharing Your Life Mission Every Day (Evangelism)

Surrendering Your Life to God's Pleasure (Worship)

SHARING CHRIST TOGETHER

six sessions on
Evangelism

written by
BRETT and **DEE EASTMAN**
TODD and **DENISE WENDORFF**
KAREN LEE-THORP

ZONDERVAN™

GRAND RAPIDS, MICHIGAN 49530 USA

We want to hear from you. Please send your comments about this book to us in care of zreview@zondervan.com. Thank you.

ZONDERVAN™

Sharing Christ Together
Copyright © 2005 by Brett and Deanna Eastman, Todd and Denise Wendorff, and Karen Lee-Thorp

Requests for information should be addressed to:

Zondervan, *Grand Rapids, Michigan 49530*

ISBN 0-310-24983-X

Interior icons by Tom Clark

Interior design by Beth Shagene & Michelle Espinoza

Printed in the United States of America

05 06 07 08 09 10 11 /❖ DCI/ 10 9 8 7 6 5 4 3 2 1

CONTENTS

EXPERIENCING CHRIST TOGETHER

EXPERIENCING CHRIST TOGETHER: LIVING WITH PURPOSE IN COMMUNITY will take you face to face with Jesus himself. In addition to being the Son of God and Savior of the world, Jesus holds the greatest wisdom and understands the purposes for which God formed you. He knows what it takes to build authentic relationships, to know God more intensely, to grow spiritually, and ultimately to make a difference in the world. EXPERIENCING CHRIST TOGETHER offers you a chance to do what Jesus' first followers did: spend time with him, listen to what he said, watch what he did, and pattern your life after his.

Jesus lived every moment following God's purpose for his life. In this study you will experience firsthand how he did this and how you can do it too. Yet if you're anything like us, knowing what God wants for you is one thing, but doing it is something else. That's why you'll follow Jesus' plan of doing life not alone but together. As you follow in his footsteps, you'll find his pathway more exciting than anything you've imagined.

Book 1 of this series (*Beginning in Christ Together*) explores the person of Jesus Christ. Each of the subsequent five studies looks through Jesus' eyes at one of God's five biblical purposes for his people (fellowship, discipleship, service, evangelism, and worship). For example, *Sharing Christ Together* deals with evangelism. Book 1 is about grace: what Christ has done for us. The other books are about how we live in response to grace.

Even if you've done another LIFE TOGETHER study, you'll be amazed at how Jesus can take you to places of faith you've never been before. The joy of life in him is far beyond a life you could design on your own. If you do all six study guides in this series, you'll spend one astonishing year with Jesus Christ.

Jesus' Heart for the Lost

Have you ever gone driving in an unfamiliar place and realized you were lost? Being lost is frustrating and sometimes scary. Sometimes we don't even know we're lost until we're so far offtrack that we're in trouble.

That's what life is like for millions of people. They're lost. Some know they're lost, and they feel frustrated or scared. Others would take offense if you hinted they didn't know where they were going.

If you've known Christ for many years, you may sometimes forget what it was like to navigate life without the Bible, the Holy Spirit, and God's people. You may get impatient at others for the choices they make. You may prefer to spend time with people who generally agree with you about which way is north.

Jesus didn't feel that way. He knew immeasurably more than we do about how to travel through life and where Home was. Yet he chose to spend his time among people who had no idea. He *cared* about those who were lost.

He asks us to do what he did: help lost people learn how to navigate through life and find their way Home. It doesn't matter that our map-reading skills aren't perfect yet. As long as we know a little more than someone else, we can gently and respectfully offer help.

This study aims to help you do three things: develop your compassion for lost people, learn some useful skills such as how to talk about spiritual things in plain language, and team up with a group to build relationships among the lost. If your life is busy, maybe that means one or two relationships. If you've ever been lost, you know what a relief it is when someone stops to offer directions.

Outline of Each Session

Most people want to live healthy, balanced spiritual lives, but few achieve this alone. And most small groups struggle to balance all of God's purposes in their meetings. Groups tend to overemphasize one of the five purposes, perhaps fellowship or discipleship. Rarely is there a healthy balance that includes evangelism, ministry, and worship. That's why we've included all of these elements in this study so you can live a healthy, balanced spiritual life over time.

A typical group session will include the following:

 CONNECTING WITH GOD'S FAMILY (FELLOWSHIP). The foundation for spiritual growth is an intimate connection with God and his family. A few people who really know you and who earn your trust provide a place to experience the life Jesus invites you to live. This section of each session typically offers you two options. You can get to know your whole group by using the icebreaker question (always question 1), or you can check in with one or two group members—your spiritual partner(s)—for a deeper connection and encouragement in your spiritual journey.

DVD TEACHING SEGMENT. A DVD companion to this study guide is available. For each study session, a teacher discusses the topic, ordinary Christians talk about the personal experience of the topic, a scholar gives background on the Bible passage, and a leadership coach gives tips to the group leader. The DVD contains worship helps and other features as well. If you are using the DVD, you will view the teaching segment after your Connecting discussion and before your Bible study (the Growing section). At the end of each session in this study guide you will find space for your notes on the teaching segment. To view a sample of the DVD, log on to www.lifetogether.com/ExperiencingChristTogether.

 GROWING TO BE LIKE CHRIST (DISCIPLESHIP). Here is where you come face to face with Christ. In a core Bible passage you'll see Jesus in action, teaching or demonstrating some aspect of how he wants you to live. The focus won't be on accumulating information but on how Jesus' words and actions relate to what you say and do. We want to help you apply the Scriptures practically, creatively, and from your heart as well as your head. At the end of the day, allowing the timeless truths from God's Word to transform our lives in Christ is our greatest aim.

FOR DEEPER STUDY. If you want to dig deeper into more Bible passages about the topic at hand, we've provided additional passages and questions. Your group may choose to do study homework ahead of each meeting in order to cover more biblical material. Or you as an individual may choose to study the For Deeper Study passages on your own. If you prefer not to do study homework, the Growing section will provide you with plenty to discuss within the group. These options allow individuals or the whole group to go deeper in their study, while still accommodating those who can't do homework or are new to your group.

You can record your discoveries on the Reflections page at the end of each session. We encourage you to read some of your insights to a friend (spiritual partner) for accountability and support. Spiritual partners may check in each week over the phone, through email, or at the beginning of the group meeting.

SHARING YOUR LIFE MISSION EVERY DAY (EVANGELISM). Many people skip over this aspect of the Christian life because it's scary, relationally awkward, or simply too much work for their busy schedules. But Jesus wanted all of his disciples to help outsiders connect with him, to know him personally. This doesn't mean preaching on street corners. It could mean welcoming a few newcomers into your group, hosting a short-term group in your home, participating in a cross-cultural missions project, or walking through this study with a friend. Throughout this study, you'll have an opportunity to take a small step in this area. These steps will take you beyond Bible study to Bible living.

SURRENDERING YOUR LIFE FOR GOD'S PLEASURE (WORSHIP). God is most pleased by a heart that is fully his. Each group session will give you a chance to surrender your heart to God in prayer and worship. You may read a psalm together, share a page in your journal, or use one of the songs on the DVD to open or close your meeting. (Additional music is available on the LIFE TOGETHER Worship DVD/CD series, produced by Maranatha!) If you've never prayed aloud in a group before, no one will put pressure on you. Instead, you'll experience the support of others who are praying for you. This time will knit your hearts in community and help you surrender all your hurts and dreams into the hands of the One who knows you best.

STUDY NOTES. This section provides background notes on the Bible passage(s) you examine in the Growing section. You may want to refer to these notes during your group meeting or as a reference for those doing additional study.

REFLECTIONS. At the end of each session is a blank page on which you can write your insights from your personal time with God. Whether you do deeper Bible study, read through the apostle Paul's letters, meditate on a few verses, or simply write out your prayers, you'll benefit from writing down what you discover. You may want to pick up a blank journal or notepad after you fill in these pages.

THE FATHER'S HEART

In the middle of a frenzied school year, a small group of women gathered week after week to grow in Christ. Marci told the group that her sister-in-law, Meg, was struggling with cancer. None of the other women knew Meg.

Marci's heart was broken over Meg. Meg had never pursued any type of relationship with God, and Marci feared her eternal destiny was hopeless. Also, the cancer was immobilizing her life.

As Marci talked about Meg, the group began to see Meg with the heart of God. Many of the women visited Meg in the hospital, read to her, and prayed for her. One woman made a poster filled with inspirational thoughts to encourage her. Another told Meg Christ loved her and died for her. Weeks passed, and Meg was released from the hospital. She decided to attend Marci's group because of the love she had received from women she didn't even know. Each week Meg learned more about who Jesus was and why he died on the cross for her.

Meg's cancer has resurfaced. Although she hasn't committed her life to Christ, she continues to learn about his love for her. "For the first time in my life," she says, "I want to see more of who Christ is and why he came, because when these women cared for me in the hospital, I saw that something in their life was different from mine. I saw a commitment to me beyond anything I had seen before."

Amazing things happen when we let ourselves feel the Father's heart for others, especially when we respond as a group.

CONNECTING WITH GOD'S FAMILY   15 min.

1. Think of one person in your life who doesn't know Christ. Briefly describe your relationship with him or her. (Close? Friendly but distant? Chilly?)

2. Whether your group is brand new or ongoing, it's always important to reflect on and review your values together. On pages 76–77 is a sample agreement with the values we've found most

useful in sustaining healthy, balanced groups. We recommend that you choose one or two values—ones you haven't previously focused on or have room to grow in—to emphasize during this study. Choose ones that will take your group to the next stage of intimacy and spiritual health.

For this study, we suggest you focus on spiritual health. Spiritual health means living all five biblical purposes of the church in your group. We've found that fellowship and Bible study are easy elements to establish in groups, but service and outreach are much harder. Yet healthy groups do all of these things! So for the next six weeks, we hope you'll emphasize *doing* things that reflect God's heart for unbelievers.

 ## GROWING TO BE LIKE CHRIST   30–40 min.

As with everything else in the Christian life, God wants evangelism to well up from within us because our hearts are taking on the character of Jesus. Just as compassion for the lost compelled Jesus, the same concern ought to compel us. God doesn't want pressured performance. He wants inner transformation that affects our thoughts, feelings, and automatic behaviors toward others.

Disciples who share their faith just because of a pep talk or nagging guilt will lose interest when progress takes time and obstacles emerge. In training his disciples, Jesus focused on their hearts so they would spend the rest of their lives spreading their faith despite intense opposition. He told stories that provoked them to understand his Father's heart. When people asked Jesus why he did something, he often told a story that explained, in effect, "I do this because this is what my Father cares about."

3. Read Luke 15:1–10. What situation prompts Jesus to tell the stories about the lost sheep and coin?

4. How do the stories explain Jesus' behavior in this situation?

5. What impression of God's heart (thoughts, passions, priorities, character) do you get from the two stories in Luke 15:1–10?

6. Read Luke 15:11–32. How would you describe the younger son's feelings and beliefs about his father at the beginning of this story?

7. What are the older son's feelings and beliefs about his father?

8. In 15:11–32, what impression do you get of the father's heart from the way he deals with:

his younger son's departure?

his younger son's return?

his older son's response?

9. These three stories are about the hearts of Jesus and the Father. Why do you suppose they are so passionate about the lost, the runaways, the sinners?

10. How do you view the lost people in your life? Is your heart similar to the Father's heart or different?

11. What hinders you from seeing people with God's heart?

FOR DEEPER STUDY

Read Jeremiah 50:6–7 and Ezekiel 34:11–31. What was God's attitude toward the lost sheep of Israel? What would it look like for you to live with that attitude toward the lost?

Read Matthew 9:9–13. Why did Jesus invest his limited time with immoral people? What would happen if you did that? What would your Christian friends think? How would it affect you and your family?

Read Galatians 2:11–21. Like Jesus, Peter and Paul were criticized by fellow Jews for eating with "sinners." How did Peter handle the criticism? How did Paul? How would you handle such criticism?

SHARING YOUR LIFE MISSION EVERY DAY   10 min.

We have found that time alone with God is essential for developing a heart for the lost and sustaining it through life's ups and downs. The Bible is full of ideas about how to pray for ourselves and our friends (see Colossians 4:2–6 for example). In prayer we can tell God our fears, frustrations, and dreams, and listen for his encouragement.

For the next six weeks, we hope you'll make it your goal to cultivate your heart for the lost through personal prayer and Bible reading. Below are several ways to choose from.

12. *Prayer* will stretch your heart. Who are the lost sheep and wandering sons and daughters in your life? Think of family members, neighbors, work associates, your friends, your kids' friends and their families, and service providers (such as store clerks or your hairdresser). The "Circles of Life" diagram on page 16 will help you think of people in various areas of your life. Prayerfully write down at least three or four names in the circles.
Here are two options for prayer during this study:

☐ Commit to praying for these people throughout this study, both with your group and on your own. Also, ask God to show you his heart toward them. Write notes in your calendar to remind you to pray.

☐ For a deeper experience, fast and pray for someone on your prayer list. If you've never fasted before, skip one meal and spend at least twenty minutes in prayer during that time. Allow your hunger to remind you how hungry the lost son felt before he left his pig-keeping job and went home to his father (Luke 15:16–17). Ask God to increase your spiritual hunger, and the hunger of the person for whom you're praying.

CIRCLES OF LIFE

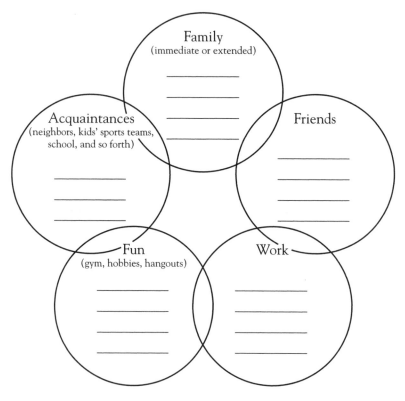

13. *Studying, meditating, and journaling on the Scriptures* also will stretch your heart. Here are two options for personal interaction with the Scriptures.

☐ **Bible Reading.** In the next six weeks, read five New Testament letters to see what they say about sharing your life with the lost. Use the Bible Reading Plan on page 89 if you like. We recommend that you jot down your thoughts on the Reflections page or in a journal.

☐ **Meditation.** If you've read these letters before, try meditation as a way of internalizing God's Word more deeply. Copy a portion of each week's Bible study passage onto a card, and tape it somewhere in your line of sight, such as on your car's dashboard or the kitchen table. Think about it when you sit at red lights, or while you're eating a meal. What is God saying to you, here and now, through these words? Several alternative passages for meditation are suggested on the Reflections page in each session. You may use that page to write your responses to your meditation verses.

14. Pair up with someone in your group. This person will be your "spiritual partner" during this study. He or she will encourage you in developing your heart for the lost. If you have done another LIFE TOGETHER study and already have a spiritual partner, you may stay with that person or change partners.

   On pages 20–21 is a Personal Health Plan, a chart for keeping track of your progress. In the box that says, "WHO are you connecting with spiritually?" write your partner's name. In the box that says, "WHAT is your next step for growth?" write the steps you chose in questions 12 and 13. You can see that the health plan contains space for you to record the ups and downs of your progress each week, with your partner to cheer you on. There's also room to record your partner's progress.

   If you have more than one partner, an additional health plan is on pages 84–85 in the Appendix. Also, on pages 86–87 you'll find a completed health plan filled in as an example. For now, don't worry about the WHERE, WHEN, and HOW questions on the health plan.

15. One great way to share your life is to invite someone to join this group. Who do you know who would benefit from your small group?

SURRENDERING YOUR LIFE FOR GOD'S PLEASURE 15–30 min.

16. Prayer aligns our vision with God's. God longs for us to ask him to do things that reflect his heart, because such prayers open avenues for him to work. The Bible is full of ideas for this kind of prayer. From Luke 15 you might pray:

   • That God will search for your friend the way a shepherd searches for a lost sheep
   • That God will use the circumstances in your friend's life to help him realize that life apart from God doesn't satisfy him, the way the lost son "came to his senses" when he was hungry (Luke 15:17)

- That God will fill you with the compassion the father feels for the lost son (Luke 15:20)

Take some time to pray for yourselves and for the lost persons in your lives.

STUDY NOTES

Sinners (Luke 15:1–2). The teachers of the law had traditions that spelled out how to live in obedience to God's law. Their intention (obedience to God) was admirable, but the traditions had the unfortunate effect of making it impossible for whole classes of people to live as observant Jews. Shepherds were classed as impure because they handled dead carcasses and couldn't pay for cleansing rituals afterward. Tax collecting was as disreputable a career as loan sharking or prostitution. Jesus spent his time among such people and got the same reaction that we might get if we spent our time with prostitutes and drug dealers. Do you fear being judged by fellow Christians for the company you keep?

Lost sheep (15:4). Jesus agreed with the Pharisees that tax collectors, prostitutes, and others had wandered away from God like sheep (Isaiah 53:6; Jeremiah 50:6). His disagreement was about how to deal with the strays: Condemn them or pursue them? Ezekiel 34:11–31 described God seeking his lost sheep and caring for them, offering protection and nourishment. Though God's sheep have wandered, he deeply loves them and will seek them until they are found. In fact, God says he desires none to perish (2 Peter 3:9; 1 Timothy 2:4).

Give me my share of the estate (15:12). No son in Jesus' day would have been so pretentious as to ask for his inheritance before his father's death. Any father would have kicked out his son without a dime. Jesus chose an extreme, preposterous example to show our hearts and the Father's heart. We are like children who wish our Father God dead so we can spend "our" resources as we please. The Father loves us despite this appalling attitude.

Wild living (15:13). We call this the story of the prodigal son because of the son's wild living. "Prodigal" means overzealous and recklessly extravagant. Yet the father was prodigal too. He waited overzealously for his son's return, then threw an extravagant party. We could call this the story of the prodigal father.

PERSONAL HEALTH PLAN

This worksheet could become your single most important feature in this study. On it you can record your personal priorities before the Father. It will help you live a healthy spiritual life, balancing all five of God's purposes.

PURPOSE	PLAN
CONNECT	WHO are you connecting with spiritually?
GROW	WHAT is your next step for growth?
DEVELOP	WHERE are you serving?
SHARE	WHEN are you shepherding another in Christ?
SURRENDER	HOW are you surrendering your heart?

If you have more than one partner, another Personal Health Plan can be found in the Appendix or downloaded in a larger format at www.lifeto-gether.com/healthplan. A Sample Health Plan is also in the Appendix.

DATE	MY PROGRESS	PARTNER'S PROGRESS

PRAYER AND PRAISE REPORT

Briefly share your prayer requests with the large group, making notations below. Then gather in smaller groups of two to four to pray for each other.

Date: _____

Prayer Requests

_____

_____

_____

_____

_____

_____

_____

_____

_____

_____

Praise Report

_____

_____

_____

_____

_____

_____

_____

_____

_____

_____

REFLECTIONS

Use this page to write out your prayers, your thoughts about your daily Bible reading, or your meditations on a verse from the passage you have already studied. Below are some suggested verses for meditation. The Bible Reading Plan is on page 89.

For Meditation: Luke 15:7, 15:20–24, or 15:31–32

For Bible Reading:

- What is the gospel Paul wants to communicate?

- How does Paul want his readers to treat unbelievers?

DVD NOTES

If you are watching the accompanying *Sharing Christ Together* DVD, write down what you sense God saying to you through the speaker. (If you'd like to hear a sample of the DVD teaching segment, go to www.lifetogether.com/ ExperiencingChristTogether.)

CHRIST IN FLESH AND BLOOD

Barbara can't drive because of a disability. Several caregivers assist her at home, and one of them drives her to church. Over the years, Barbara has come to see her disability not as an annoying limitation but as an opportunity for ministry. For instance, because Barbara can't drive, a caregiver who wouldn't attend church on her own must go weekly. And Barbara's church is the kind of place that gets an unbeliever's attention.

But effective Sunday services alone might not transform a caregiver's heart. Barbara herself is key.

Consider Alison. When Alison first started working for Barbara several years ago, she had just separated from her husband. Through kindness, Barbara earned Alison's trust. Alison told Barbara she didn't want to live anymore. But while Alison went through her daily tasks of cleaning, transporting, and caring for Barbara, she saw how Barbara dealt with her disability, treated people, and relied on God. Watching Barbara, Alison saw a God of love, forgiveness, hope, and strength. Alison saw Barbara grateful for what she called miracles in her life—not the miracle of complete healing, but the mundane miracles of daily provision. Alison came to love God, and when Barbara began to host a small group in her home, Alison joined.

When God wanted to offer his love to a lost world, he came in the flesh, in Jesus Christ. He is still present in the flesh in people like Barbara, people like you.

CONNECTING WITH GOD'S FAMILY   10 min.

Take a few minutes either to connect as a whole group (question 1) or to let spiritual partners connect one-on-one (question 2).

1. Finish this sentence: "This week, God ..."

☐ Laughed at me because ...
☐ Encouraged me by ...
☐ Convicted me because ...
☐ Blessed me with ...

☐ Showed me . . .
☐ Taught me . . .
☐ Challenged me to . . .

Or,

2. Sit with your spiritual partner(s). If you partner is absent, join with another individual or pair. Share something from your journal, Bible reading, or prayer time. What has God been saying to you? What have you been saying to God?

GROWING TO BE LIKE CHRIST   30 min.

How did Christ spread the good news of God? "The Word became flesh and made his dwelling among us" (John 1:14). *Christ himself* was the message. His life said what God wanted us to hear. He became one of us and moved into our neighborhood. We can learn a great deal about our own role in the world from studying his example.

The apostle Paul calls us "the body of Christ" (1 Corinthians 12:27). Together, we are the in-the-flesh presence of Christ in our world. We are here to dwell among unbelievers so they too can become children of God. We do what Jesus did. Jesus wasn't afraid to be contaminated (Matthew 9:10–13), offended, rejected, or bored by sinful people. He was "full of grace and truth" (John 1:14) when he interacted with them. We need the same graceful, truthful hearts toward the world that he had when he lived here on earth.

3. Read John 1:1–14. What do you learn about Christ from verses 1–5? (See also the Study Notes on page 31.)

4. What were Christ's goals in becoming flesh and dwelling among us (verses 9–14)?

5. What do you think it cost him to become flesh and dwell among us? (You might want to check out Philippians 2:5–10, especially verses 5–8.)

6. Why couldn't his goals have been accomplished without this drastic decision to live as a human in our midst?

7. How, in practice, do we go about being Christ's in-the-flesh presence among unbelievers? What insights do you gain from Jesus' teaching in the following passages?

Luke 6:27–38

Matthew 9:9–13

Matthew 5:47

John 13:34–35

8. Why would this kind of behavior be effective in drawing unbelievers to consider the gospel?

9. What does it cost us to treat others in these ways?

10. Which of the behaviors mentioned above do you find most challenging as you live as Christ's presence among unbelievers?

FOR DEEPER STUDY

Read Matthew 4:17–25. What does it mean to be a fisher of men? How does Jesus equip a person for that task?

Think about Philippians 2:5–10 (question 5). What difference does it make to you that Jesus was willing to pay this cost for you?

Read the larger context in Philippians 2:1–16. How would the attitudes and behavior Paul describes draw unbelievers to faith in Christ? Which of these attitudes or behaviors would make the most difference to unbelievers in your life, if they saw you like this? How do you think a person grows in these habits?

11. Where are you already living among unbelievers? That's your mission field! Look back at the "Circles of Life" diagram on page 16. Add any additional names that come to mind from your workplace, your children's after-school activities, your neighborhood, your gym. If you don't know someone's name, write "the parent who is always at my daughter's soccer matches."

12. Below is a list of habits based on Jesus' instructions. Choose one that isn't already second nature to you, and tell your spiritual partner (or the person sitting next to you) which one you chose. Then make a point of practicing this habit for the next week. Jot notes about this experience on your Reflections page (page 34).

☐ Greet people who are not your friends, including receptionists, store clerks, janitors—anybody you come across. How easily do a smile and a greeting come to your lips?

☐ If you regularly encounter a particular person, such as the cashier at your favorite coffee house, ask his or her name. Write down the name so you can greet this person by name next time.

☐ When you are in the wrong, apologize to the other person. (Don't choose this one if you are a compulsive apologizer! Choose it if you rarely apologize.)

☐ When someone else offends you, offer mercy instead of judgment.

☐ Be generous, especially to those who don't deserve it.

☐ When you say you'll do something, follow through.

☐ Tell the truth, even when shading the truth would be to your advantage.

☐ Go out of your way to be kind to someone you don't like, or who doesn't like you.

☐ Offer hospitality to someone who isn't already your friend and who isn't in a position to do something for you. This doesn't have to be elaborate; you could simply invite a coworker to lunch.

☐ Take time to listen to people.

☐ Serve people: Help them with their coat or bring them a cold drink. Make a point of holding doors open for people, letting others enter an elevator ahead of you, or inviting someone with a few items to get in the store checkout line ahead of you.

13. You will be Christ-in-the-flesh much more effectively as a group than individually. We have found that the healthiest groups do outreach projects at least every few months. Ask for two volunteers to plan an outreach event your group can do in the next sixty days. Here are a few examples:

☐ Have a family barbecue, theme dinner, block party, women's coffee, or men's sports night. Invite non-Christians. Make sure there are at least as many unchurched guests as there are members of your group. Don't worry about making a gospel presentation, especially if you don't already have solid friendships with these unbelievers. Just love them and serve them. We call this a "Matthew party" because of Matthew 9:9–13.

☐ If you live in a snowy area, plan a morning to shovel snow for elderly neighbors.

☐ Offer to rake leaves or do other yard work.

☐ Hold a neighborhood car wash, and emphasize that it's free and you don't want anybody's money. Tell them service is a spiritual exercise for your group, and they'll be doing you a favor if they let you wash their car.

Turn to the Personal Health Plan on pages 20–21. Under "WHEN are you shepherding another in Christ?" write a step you plan to take in this area.

SURRENDERING YOUR LIFE FOR GOD'S PLEASURE   15 min.

14. Gather into circles of two or three people so that everyone has time to share and pray. Let everyone answer this question: "How can we pray for you this week?" Write down requests in the Prayer and Praise Report on page 33.

Pray for these requests, as well as for the unbelievers whose names you listed in your "Circles of Life" diagram. Pray about your responses to questions 11–13 above. Ask God to give you loving, servant hearts so you can be his in-the-flesh presence in your daily lives.

STUDY NOTES

Jesus expected his disciples to teach and do what he taught and did. He prayed for them: "My prayer is not that you take them out of the world but that you protect them from the evil one. . . . As you sent me into the world, I have sent them into the world" (John 17:15, 18). He left them on earth to be God's message on his behalf.

The Word (John 1:1). In Greek culture, *logos* meant more than spoken words. It meant personality expressed in communication. Jesus embodied the very heart and character of God as he spoke the words of God. *Logos* also meant the embodiment of what was true and real. It was "the rational mind that ruled the universe."[1] To a Hebrew thinker, the *logos* of God was the word by which God spoke the universe into existence, and God's fullest self-expression. Jesus was both the full expression of the Old Testament God and the embodiment of what was true, real, and rational. Some false religions use this passage to indicate that Jesus was just "a god," not *the* God. The original Greek grammar and syntax decisively indicate that he was one with God and equal with all the qualities of God.

Darkness has not understood it (1:5). Darkness finds light mystifying. It's no wonder that people who have grown up in darkness have trouble understanding us if we simply tell them about Christ. It takes much more than our words to convince people accustomed to darkness that it's worth giving up darkness for what we have.

His own did not receive him (1:11). Jesus first came to the Jewish nation, and most of them rejected him (Matthew 23:37). His own were Jews living in Israel/Palestine.

---

[1] "John," *The Expositor's Bible Commentary, New Testament*, Frank E. Gaebelein, gen. ed., in Zondervan Reference Software, version 2.8 (Grand Rapids: Zondervan, 1998).

Children of God (1:12). Some today teach that all humans are children of God. Though it's true that God created all of us in his image and for his purpose, Ephesians 2:3–5 says humans are by nature children of wrath, spiritually dead because of our deeply rooted inclination to sin. Only through faith in Christ are we reunited with God and adopted as his children (Ephesians 1:5; Galatians 3:26–4:7).

Word became flesh (1:14). Christ—the self-expression and creative power of the Old Testament God, the embodiment of truth and reality—became fully human. Jesus was human physically, mentally, and in every other way. His nature was sinless and perfect, while ours is not, but he experienced temptation to sin. He got hungry and tired. He experienced life as a poor person in what we would call an underdeveloped country. Yet he retained his deity. He was still the Word of God. He revealed God's glory—God's radiant character.

PRAYER AND PRAISE REPORT

Briefly share your prayer requests with the large group, making notations below. Then gather in smaller groups of two to four to pray for each other.

Date: _____

Prayer Requests

_____

_____

_____

_____

_____

_____

_____

_____

_____

_____

Praise Report

_____

_____

_____

_____

_____

_____

_____

_____

_____

_____

_____

REFLECTIONS

Use this page to write out your prayers, your thoughts about your daily Bible reading, or your meditations on a verse from the passage you have already studied. Below are some suggested verses for meditation. The Bible Reading Plan is on page 89.

For Meditation: John 1:14, Matthew 5:47, or Luke 6:32–36

For Bible Reading:

• What is the gospel Paul wants to communicate?

• How does Paul want his readers to treat unbelievers?

DVD NOTES

If you are watching the accompanying *Sharing Christ Together* DVD, write down what you sense God saying to you through the speaker. (If you'd like to hear a sample of the DVD teaching segment, go to www.lifetogether.com/ExperiencingChristTogether.)

SOWING SEEDS

Trevor grew up in a Christian home, going to church every Sunday. He knew the gospel, and he believed it. But when it came to sharing his faith with others, he never really gave it much thought. In his mind, explaining the gospel to someone who wasn't a believer was something only "super spiritual" people did.

When Trevor went to college, he began to meet guys who were really serious about their relationship with God. These guys were highly committed to studying the Bible, praying, and sharing their beliefs with others. When Trevor got involved in a small group with some of them, he was challenged by their genuine love for God and the way it showed up in their lifestyles.

The more time he spent with them, the more impressed he became with their desire to share the gospel with others, and the more he began to think about why he didn't share their passion. *If I believe what I say,* he thought, *that means there are people I know who are going to hell. Shouldn't I feel more of an urgency to share the truth with them?*

While Trevor still felt uncomfortable thinking how he would explain the gospel to someone, he decided to at least pray about it. "God," he said, "if you want me to do this, increase my desire and show me how to do it."

The very next afternoon, Trevor was hanging out in his dorm room when his small group leader knocked on his door.

"Hey Trevor," said Brandon, "there are a couple of guys down the hall I've been spending time with, and I think they're ready to have a conversation about the gospel. Do you want to come with me? You don't have to say anything if you don't want to. You can just listen."

Brandon already had developed friendships with these guys, and Trevor was amazed how the conversation about spiritual matters flowed naturally out of the existing relationship. Though Trevor didn't say much, he began to think differently about the nature of sharing his faith.

CONNECTING WITH GOD'S FAMILY   10 min.

If we think of faith in Christ as a large tree that grows in a person's life over time, we can imagine everything we say about faith to an unbeliever as a seed. Jesus rarely explained his entire message to someone at one time. He understood that a person would be overwhelmed. Instead, he planted seeds—small pieces of his message—and gave them time to sprout.

One of the most important ways we can sow seeds of the gospel in a person's life is to discuss common human experiences. These subjects naturally lead to spiritual conversations that are neither preachy nor religious. These conversations may not contain the whole gospel at one time. They are simply seeds, and it's God's job to make them grow.

1. Choose one of the following, and briefly tell how you've experienced it during the past week:

   ☐ Love
   ☐ Hope
   ☐ Joy
   ☐ Loneliness
   ☐ Disappointment
   ☐ Broken relationship
   ☐ Death

GROWING TO BE LIKE CHRIST   30 min.

Jesus' original audience was full of farmers and fishermen, so it's not surprising that he told stories about farm life and fishing to illustrate his central point: "Repent, for the kingdom of heaven is near" (Matthew 4:17). He was a genius at discussing spiritual realities in familiar, nonreligious language. His message, methods, and mind-set are all excellent examples of how to sow seeds.

2. Read Matthew 13:1–23. In Jesus' story, the seed represents God's Word. How would you evaluate the sower's method of sowing? Would you call it wasteful? Please explain your view.

3. When he talked to the crowds, why did Jesus talk about spiritual reality through stories, rather than explaining straightforwardly that he was the Son of God, that people were sinners, and that they needed to trust him for salvation (verses 10–17)?

4. Why do you think Jesus bothered scattering the seed of the Word among the crowds, where so much of the seed would fail to take root and grow?

5. Why didn't Jesus feel crushed when so many people rejected him and his message?

6. What obstacles need to be overcome in the soil of a person's heart in order for the seed to bear fruit?

7. Imagine that you talk about spiritual things with fifty people. Twenty-five of them have hearts as hard as the path: they're not even interested in spiritual realities. Fifteen of them are like rocky soil: they go to church with you for a while and say they love it, but when God doesn't make their lives easy, they decide he's not worth their time. Eight people become consistent churchgoers, but chasing "the good life" is the main thing on their minds. Only two out of those fifty people become faithful, fruitful followers of Christ.

How would you handle that? Would you:

☐ Feel rejected by the twenty-five?

☐ Feel hurt by the fifteen?

☐ Get frustrated at the eight?

☐ Blame yourself?

☐ Feel good about having been faithful to sow seeds, regardless of the outcome?

☐ Give up?

☐ Persevere?

FOR DEEPER STUDY

Read Isaiah 6:8–13, in which God gives the prophet Isaiah his life assignment. What was Isaiah's assignment? Why do you suppose God gave him an assignment to proclaim the truth to people who God knew wouldn't listen? What does this passage have to do with Matthew 13?

Read Jeremiah 4:3. What does Jeremiah mean by "break up your unplowed ground"? How do you think a person goes about doing this? How can friends help?

Ezekiel 2:3–7 describes the prophet Ezekiel's assignment. How is it like Isaiah's? How is it like Jesus'? How is it like yours?

What can we learn from Jesus' example?

- We can scatter the seeds of spiritual truth broadly, without unrealistic expectations and without taking it personally if many don't respond.
- We can learn to talk about spiritual truth in the common language of our culture, at a level appropriate to the person we're talking to.
- We can recognize that different people's hearts are resistant in different ways, and we can turn to God in prayer to soften hard soil and remove the stones and thorns.

Talking about spiritual things in ordinary language is a skill you can learn with practice. For example, say that tomorrow your unchurched coworker asks, "What did you do last night?" You could respond:

- ☐ "Not much." (This is the chicken way out. It's evasive if not outright untrue.)
- ☐ "I went to a Bible study. We studied how Jesus spread the gospel, and we prayed for our non-Christian friends." (This is honest but possibly unintelligible to those who don't even know what the word "gospel" means. Also, it makes you sound religious in a way that might make an unbeliever less curious, rather than more curious, about your spiritual life.)
- ☐ "I have this group of friends that meets weekly to talk about how we can live with more meaning and purpose. It's great to have some people who care about my becoming a better person." (This is also honest but will provoke much more positive curiosity. If answers like this don't naturally spring to your mind, it's worth thinking ahead of time how you can answer common questions such as "What did you do last night?")

8. Gather into smaller circles of two or three people. Without using language that would confuse or offend someone who doesn't go to church, talk to your partners about one of the following:

☐ Something in your life that God is helping you with
☐ What you do in this group
☐ Something you're praying about
☐ Something you have recently learned from the Bible

Give each other feedback and plenty of encouragement. This is a hard skill at first, especially for those who have been attending church for a long time!

9. Allow a few minutes for the persons planning your outreach event (session 2, question 13) to report on progress and solicit any needed help.

 SURRENDERING YOUR LIFE FOR GOD'S PLEASURE 15–30 min.

Jesus teaches us how to pray for unbelievers. For example, the story of the four soils suggests what we can ask God to do in the hearts of different people: soften hard soil, break up rocks that keep the seed from sinking deeply in, tear up thorns, and help seekers past obstacles such as the reason for suffering or the allure of "the good life."

Another valuable passage is John 16:7–11. Here Jesus explains that it's the Holy Spirit's job to convince people that they are sinners, that unbelief is the root of sin, that Jesus alone is righteous, and that God will judge each person. What great news: it's not our job to convince people that they're sinners! We don't have to tell them what's wrong with their sexual behavior, for instance, unless they genuinely ask for our opinion. We can simply go to God and ask him to do the convicting. Karen has seen this work over and over: a friend realizing that his behavior is actually what the Bible would call sin.

10. In your smaller circles, take a few minutes to pray for the unbelievers in your lives. Use Matthew 13:1–23 and John 16:7–11 for ideas on what to pray.

11. In a conversation with an unbeliever, listening is perhaps even more important than talking. You can practice your listening skills here in this group. Allow everyone to answer this question: "How can we pray for you this week?" As people share,

practice listening closely rather than thinking about what you'd like to say.

Then pray for these requests. Ask God to give you faithful servant hearts as you scatter the seed of the Word.

STUDY NOTES

Sow (Matthew 13:3). In ancient Israel, farmers sowed their seed by hand. They tossed the seed liberally to the ground, knowing that some would not fall in the best soil. They tilled the soil afterward to make the seeds sink into the dirt. Today's farmers till first and then carefully sow seed in the good, tilled soil, but that wasn't the method in Jesus' day. To us, scattering seed on hard ground seems wasteful, and talking about spiritual things with hard-hearted people may seem wasteful too. But Jesus values generous liberality, not efficiency.

Seed (13:3). The gospel, the message about God's kingdom and how to enter it, is the seed. When received, it brings about salvation.

Soil (13:5). People respond differently to the gospel. Depending on the condition of their hearts, they may reject it, receive it superficially, or fully embrace it and let it change their lives.

A hundred . . . times what was sown (13:8). Hundredfold crop production was unheard of in first-century agriculture. Tenfold was normal. People would have thought, *What kind of seed could produce such a crop?* Fruit is the test of true salvation. Jesus said, "By their fruit you will recognize them" (Matthew 7:16–23). Abundant fruit, not words, is a sign of a true believer.

Secrets of the kingdom of heaven (13:11). Jesus taught in parables to pique people's curiosity and sort out those who were idly curious from those who really wanted to understand God's kingdom. Those who truly wanted to know (the disciples, for example) pursued Jesus for more information.

Similarly, we might have a conversation with an unbeliever about an everyday issue, say disappointment. We might mention how our faith helps us handle disappointment. If the other person is interested in spiritual things, he or she will pursue that line of discussion. If not, there's no point in our giving a lecture on the hope of eternal life available through faith in Jesus Christ, who died for our sins.

Otherwise they might see (13:15). The interplay between God's sovereignty and humans' responsibility to choose sometimes confuses us. Does God deliberately withhold the capacity for spiritual sight from some people, knowing that the consequences will be disastrous for them? Or do people choose spiritual blindness, and God simply lets them have what they want? It's not either/or; it's both. We may not like paradox, but God does.

PRAYER AND PRAISE REPORT

Briefly share your prayer requests with the large group, making notations below. Then gather in smaller groups of two to four to pray for each other.

Date: _____

Prayer Requests

_____

_____

_____

_____

_____

_____

_____

_____

_____

_____

Praise Report

_____

_____

_____

_____

_____

_____

_____

_____

_____

_____

REFLECTIONS

Use this page to write out your prayers, your thoughts about your daily Bible reading, or your meditations on a verse from the passage you have already studied. Below are some suggested verses for meditation. The Bible Reading Plan is on page 89.

For Meditation: Matthew 13:3–9 or 13:18–23

For Bible Reading:

- What is the gospel Paul wants to communicate?

- How does Paul want his readers to treat unbelievers?

DVD NOTES

If you are watching the accompanying *Sharing Christ Together* DVD, write down what you sense God saying to you through the speaker. (If you'd like to hear a sample of the DVD teaching segment, go to www.lifetogether.com/ ExperiencingChristTogether.)

_____

_____

_____

_____

_____

_____

_____

_____

_____

_____

_____

_____

_____

_____

_____

_____

_____

_____

_____

_____

_____

_____

_____

_____

_____

WHO IS MY NEIGHBOR?

Evie didn't understand why David felt shy being the only Chinese-American in a small group full of Anglo-Americans. She thought of David as a person, not as Chinese. Then David and his girlfriend got engaged, and Evie and her husband were invited to the rehearsal dinner. David's large Chinese family was all there. The food was Chinese, and Evie felt what it was like to be the minority.

Not long after, the daughter of one of Evie's coworkers turned fifteen. In Mexican culture, a daughter's fifteenth birthday called for a celebration that reminded Evie of a wedding. Evie found herself at a party where almost everyone but her spoke both Spanish and English, and where the customs were unfamiliar to her. Once again, she felt shy.

Both her coworker's Mexican family and David's Chinese family made a point of making Evie and her husband feel welcome in their midst. Evie decided that she needed to make a point of offering hospitality to people different from her. She was thrilled some months later when David commented on how comfortable their small group had become. Now that an Indian/Anglo family and a Mexican/Anglo family were also members, his shyness had melted.

Cross-cultural outreach can feel awkward at first, but it's an essential part of sharing our lives with the world.

CONNECTING WITH GOD'S FAMILY   10 min.

Begin either by having the group think about the topic of this session (question 1) or by giving spiritual partners a chance to check in with each other (question 2).

1. Recall a positive interaction you have had with someone from an ethnic group different from your own. Take one minute to share part of the story with the group.

   Or,

2. Sit with your spiritual partner. Share something from your journal, your Bible reading, or your prayers for unbelieving friends. How can your partner pray for you?

 GROWING TO BE LIKE CHRIST   30 min.

It's normal to prefer to spend time with people like ourselves. Similarity makes us comfortable. Persons from other ethnic groups may speak with accents we struggle to understand, or eat food we don't care for, or have customs that bewilder us. Those without church backgrounds may never have heard of our favorite author or radio program or recording artist. They may not understand what we mean by seemingly obvious words like "sin" or "truth." Their political or social views may seem destructive to us, and if we base our views on biblical principles, our reasoning may make no sense to them.

Socializing and communicating across a cultural divide takes work—and our lives are already stressful. Yet Jesus encourages us to widen our view and notice needs among persons who may be very different from us.

3. Read Luke 10:25–37. What prompts Jesus to tell the story about the man attacked on the road?

4. How is Jesus' question in verse 36 different from the legal expert's original question in verse 29?

5. What do you think is the point of Jesus' story?

6. Read the study note for "Samaritan" on page 52. Why do you think Jesus chose a Samaritan to be the good guy in this story?

7. If Jesus told this story at your church, which ethnic group or type of person might he choose to be the outsider, the Samaritan?

8. The Samaritan crossed a cultural line to be a neighbor to a person in need. What factors sometimes hinder us from caring about—or even knowing about—the physical and spiritual needs of people from other cultures?

9. What are some ways we might overcome these cultural barriers?

10. What does this parable motivate you to do?

FOR DEEPER STUDY

Read the original context of "love your neighbor" in Leviticus 19:13–18. What various ways of loving one's neighbor does Leviticus list? How would it be different to live in a society where you were expected to treat only your own ethnic group like this?

Read Proverbs 14:21. If you despise a neighbor, how could you deal with that person differently?

How would you answer the questions Jesus asks in Matthew 5:46–47? Why do you think he makes such a big deal about this?

What motivations for cross-cultural outreach do you find in 2 Corinthians 5:14–21? In James 2:8–11?

 SHARING YOUR LIFE MISSION EVERY DAY   20 min.

Jesus commissioned his followers to be his representatives "in Jerusalem [their immediate neighborhood], and in all Judea and Samaria [their region, populated by many ethnic groups], and to the ends of the earth" (Acts 1:8). That mandate applies not just to a few of us, but to all of us working together.

11. What opportunities do you—individually and as a group—have to address the physical or spiritual needs in other cultures? Think about the people who are culturally or ethnically different from you close to home, as well as those in other countries.

12. Choose one of the following ideas to do as a group, or follow through on one of your own ideas. Ask one or two group members to organize this effort.

☐ Have a dinner or party and invite one or more persons from another culture.

☐ If you have a college campus nearby, contact the office that handles international students and find out how you can help those students feel welcome in your country.

☐ Walk through a neighborhood that is ethnically different from yours, and pray for the people who live there.

☐ Choose a missionary (perhaps with your pastor's help), and write to him or her.

☐ Consider supporting a missionary financially as a group.

SURRENDERING YOUR LIFE FOR GOD'S PLEASURE 15–30 min.

13. On the Reflections page (page 54), take a moment to write a few sentences to God on what you think about cross-cultural outreach. Is it awkward for you or no big deal? Turn your thoughts into a prayer.

14. How can the group pray for you this week? Share what you wrote on your Reflections page if you feel comfortable doing so. Remember to pray also for the unbelievers in your lives.

STUDY NOTES

Paul said the love of Christ compels us to recognize others not by status, color, race, or any other manmade division, but through the eyes of Jesus (2 Corinthians 5:14–21; Galatians 3:28).

Who is my neighbor? (Luke 10:29). Jesus said all of life is summed up in how we love God and neighbor. The traditional

Jewish interpretation of "neighbor" was a fellow Jew, but Jesus' story illustrated why that interpretation was inadequate.

From Jerusalem to Jericho (10:30). That road was dangerous. It passed through desert country, steep gorges, and sharp rocks. One slip could cost your life. Also, it was a likely place to be robbed. No population or police were around. You were on your own.

Priest . . . Levite (10:31–32). The priest and Levite were Jews who worked at the temple and strictly followed the ritual laws. If they touched a corpse, a non-Jew, or anyone else unclean by the law's standards, they would be unable to do their jobs until they went through ritual cleansing. That would cost money and effort. However, Jewish tradition highly valued hospitality to strangers, and most rabbis would have said this tradition superceded the laws of cleanness in this case. The average Jew would have expected the priest and Levite to choose kindness over purity.

Samaritan (10:33). The average Jew would *not* have expected a Samaritan to be more hospitable than a religious Jew. Samaritans were descended from Jews who had stayed in Israel during the exile many centuries earlier. They had intermarried with non-Jews, so full-blood Jews considered them tainted. They had religious practices that Jews considered heretical. The tension between Jews and Samaritans in Jesus' day was similar to the tension between Jewish Israelis and Palestinian Arabs today.

Pity (10:33). "Compassion" in the New American Standard Bible. Compassion is a deep sense of concern that motivates one to take action and alleviate pain in another person's life.

PRAYER AND PRAISE REPORT

Briefly share your prayer requests with the large group, making notations below. Then gather in smaller groups of two to four to pray for each other.

Date: _____

Prayer Requests

_____

_____

_____

_____

_____

_____

_____

_____

_____

_____

Praise Report

_____

_____

_____

_____

_____

_____

_____

_____

_____

_____

REFLECTIONS

Use this page to write out your prayers, your thoughts about your daily Bible reading, or your meditations on a verse from the passage you have already studied. Below are some suggested verses for meditation. The Bible Reading Plan is on page 89.

For Meditation: Luke 10:31, 10:33–35, or 10:36–37

For Bible Reading:

- What is the gospel Paul wants to communicate?

- How does Paul want his readers to treat unbelievers?

DVD NOTES

If you are watching the accompanying *Sharing Christ Together* DVD, write down what you sense God saying to you through the speaker. (If you'd like to hear a sample of the DVD teaching segment, go to www.lifetogether.com/ExperiencingChristTogether.)

_____

_____

_____

_____

_____

_____

_____

_____

_____

_____

_____

_____

_____

_____

_____

_____

_____

_____

_____

_____

_____

_____

_____

_____

_____

_____

_____

SESSION 5

TEAMING UP

During their early years in business, Paul and John worked at the same office and talked often about their common desire to share their faith with others. It helped to have a friend for encouragement, because on many days they felt beaten down by the world and were sure they weren't making a difference. But as they swapped dreams and ideas, they decided to invite some male colleagues to have breakfast with them every Friday. At breakfast, they talked about the Bible and their faith in Christ. They let the other men ask questions and challenge their faith. Together, Paul and John were strong enough to withstand some coworker ridicule for having such an offensive meeting. They slowly gained a foothold, and a few of the men in the office came to Christ. They even had opportunities to share their faith with support staff. As others joined them, they felt that Christ himself had called them to share their faith in their town.

God never asked us to face the world on our own. In this session you'll consider how Jesus' practice of sending his disciples out in teams might work for you.

CONNECTING WITH GOD'S FAMILY   10 min.

Choose one of these opening exercises:

1. Have you had a chance to talk about spiritual realities (hope, disappointment, something you're praying about, something God is doing in your life) with an unbeliever in the past couple of weeks? If so, share a little about how that conversation went. If not, what hindered you from doing so?

   Or,

2. Connect with your spiritual partner. What is happening in your personal time with God? Is there anything in your journal that you'd like to share?

GROWING TO BE LIKE CHRIST   30 min.

Many of us find it scary to launch into a spiritual conversation all by ourselves. We're so afraid of blowing it that our minds go blank. But Jesus never intended most of his disciples to be solo evangelists. He expected them to make it a team effort. In fact, he said outsiders would find their message far more convincing if the outsiders could see how the disciples interacted with each other (John 13:34–35; 17:22–23). It's not surprising, then, that when he sent them out, he sent them in pairs.

3. Read Luke 10:1–12. Describe the assignment Jesus gave to seventy-two of his disciples.

4. What do you think he meant by calling them "lambs among wolves" (verse 3)? See the Study Notes on page 60.

5. Do you ever feel like a lamb among wolves? If so, what gives you that impression?

6. What do you make of the fact that Jesus first told them, "Ask the Lord of the harvest . . . to send out workers" and then told them, "Go!" (verses 2–3)? Why both "Ask" and "Go!"?

7. What made these people qualified to do what Jesus was asking of them? How might their previous experience with Jesus have helped them?

8. Verses 4–11 describe the specific ground rules for this mission (such as taking no supplies and relying on the hospitality of strangers). In what ways do you think the Lord's assignment for you is similar, and in what ways is it different?

9. What are the advantages of doing your assignment in pairs or groups, as opposed to on your own?

FOR DEEPER STUDY

Read Matthew 10:5–31. This passage is parallel to the one in Luke 10. What instructions from Jesus does Matthew add? Clearly, spreading Jesus' message was dangerous in those days. What risks do you face today? What risks are you willing to face? What reasons for not being afraid does Jesus give? How can a person know if she is persecuted for her faith or for being obnoxious and arrogant in the way she communicates?

Read John 13:34–35 and 17:22–23. What does Jesus add here about the potential of teams to communicate the gospel in ways an individual can't? Why are teams important?

SHARING YOUR LIFE MISSION EVERY DAY   20 min.

Possibly you're not ready to go on the road without luggage, as Jesus' first disciples did. But there are things you can do in pairs that will contribute to the spread of the gospel in ways you can't foresee. Following are several ideas for outreach as pairs or teams.

10. When you finish session 6 of this study, why not take a six-week break from your group to lead a new group? Pair up, and tell your pastor you're willing to lead a new group through the first book in this series, *Beginning in Christ Together*. It's suitable for seekers as well as believers. The study guide offers so much help for leaders that you can lead even if you've never done it before. During the six weeks, raise up one or two members of the new group to take over leadership when you go back to your old group.

Another option is to divide your whole group into pairs to launch three or four new groups. Invite people you know or ask your pastor for the phone numbers of church members, regular attenders, or visitors who live near you. After six weeks, return to your current group.

Celebrate even if your group sends out only one team. Support those willing persons with your prayers.

As you saw in session 1, Jesus has a heart for sheep without shepherds. Who are the sheep around you who need to get connected to a shepherd? They may be seekers, people raised Christian but not actively practicing their faith, or members of your church who don't have a small group in which to grow. If you've benefited from belonging to a group, we encourage you to give others the same opportunity.

With whom in your group can you pair up for this project?

11. Another thing you can do as a team is the outreach event you started planning in session 2 or the cross-cultural outreach you discussed in session 3. Allow some time for those who are planning those projects to update the group.

 ## SURRENDERING YOUR LIFE FOR GOD'S PLEASURE 15–30 min.

12. How can the group pray for you this week? Remember to pray for the unbelievers in your lives, as well as for group members who are thinking about taking a break to lead a new group.

STUDY NOTES

Lambs among wolves (Luke 10:3). Jesus' disciples were innocent and vulnerable. Some people, acting on Satan's behalf, would treat them harshly because of their message. The world is enemy territory. In Matthew 10:16, Jesus advised sheep among wolves to be "as shrewd as snakes and as innocent as doves." That means to be on guard, wise in how you handle yourself in the world, and careful to avoid the traps Satan has set. "Any man who takes Jesus Christ seriously becomes the target of the devil," Vance Havner often told audiences. "Most church members do not give Satan enough trouble to arouse his opposition."[2] Yet as risky as outreach is, we are ultimately safe in God's hands. Jesus said, "Even the very hairs of your head are all numbered" (Matthew 10:30).

---

[2]Vance Havner, quoted in Warren W. Wiersbe, "Luke," *The Bible Exposition Commentary* (Wheaton, Ill.: SP Publications, 1989), PC Study Bible Version 3.2, July 2001.

PRAYER AND PRAISE REPORT

Briefly share your prayer requests with the large group, making notations below. Then gather in smaller groups of two to four to pray for each other.

Date: _____

Prayer Requests

_____

_____

_____

_____

_____

_____

_____

_____

_____

_____

Praise Report

_____

_____

_____

_____

_____

_____

_____

_____

_____

_____

REFLECTIONS

Use this page to write out your prayers, your thoughts about your daily Bible reading, or your meditations on a verse from the passage you have already studied. Below are some suggested verses for meditation. The Bible Reading Plan is on page 89.

For Meditation: Luke 10:2 or 10:3

For Bible Reading:

- What is the gospel Paul wants to communicate?

- How does Paul want his readers to treat unbelievers?

DVD NOTES

If you are watching the accompanying *Sharing Christ Together* DVD, write down what you sense God saying to you through the speaker. (If you'd like to hear a sample of the DVD teaching segment, go to www.lifetogether.com/ ExperiencingChristTogether.)

SESSION 6 UP A TREE

For years Henry struggled with homosexual feelings, and more than once he acted on them. When Henry was in his late twenties, a Christian counselor and a small group of men with similar issues began to help him overcome his impulses.

Throughout his thirties, Henry wondered if he ever would get married. He found women attractive, but most only wanted to be his friend. He got engaged once, but his fiancée broke off the relationship two months before the wedding. Then he found his soul mate: Rhonda. Against his friends' advice, Henry married Rhonda within seven months of their first date. From the start the marriage was rough. During one particularly hard stretch only two years into their marriage, they separated. One night, for the first time in more than a decade, Henry acted on his homosexual desires.

Henry had never told Rhonda about his struggles, but in one counseling session he confessed to her his entire lifetime struggle with homosexual feelings and his recent behavior. She felt betrayed, and while she said she forgave him, the marriage was over. Six months later they were divorced. Broken and humiliated, Henry lost many of his church friends when they heard the story.

Perhaps more than in past generations, people around us are broken— churchgoers included. Many are children of divorce; many have been sexually active since their teens. Some have been sexually abused; others can be heard yelling at their children from next door. They may be tough survivors or eager to spill out their many personal problems. These people are complicated, and just praying to receive Christ won't change that.

While we may prefer to reach out to people who look and act like us, that wasn't Jesus' way. He singled out the messed up, the immoral, the people who were up a tree and needed help, like Zacchaeus in our study today. Ironically, those people appreciated him most of all.

CONNECTING WITH GOD'S FAMILY   10 min.

1. Share with the group one of the following:

   ☐ A highlight from your personal prayer and Bible reflection; perhaps something from your journal

   ☐ An opportunity you had this week to talk about spiritual things in ordinary language with an unbeliever

   ☐ An opportunity you had to serve an unbeliever as Christ's in-the-flesh presence

GROWING TO BE LIKE CHRIST   30 min.

Hurting people often have telltale signs of their need and desire for spiritual truth. They may smoke or drink too much. They may swear, lose their temper, cry easily, or talk nonstop. Some sample the spiritual buffet: Zen meditation, astrology, Gnosticism, angels. Others talk about how they were wounded by their parents or the church of their childhood.

It's tempting to avert our eyes when we see signs of people's brokenness. But Jesus watched for those signs and responded.

2. Read Luke 19:1–10. What do you think could have motivated a chief tax collector—a wealthy and unscrupulous man—to climb a tree to see Jesus? (You might want to refer to the study note for "chief tax collector" on page 69.)

3. Why didn't Jesus mind shocking people when he invited himself to Zacchaeus's home?

4. Why do you suppose Zacchaeus responded as he did in verse 8?

5. Jesus makes a strong statement about his life mission in verse 10. How is your life mission similar or different?

6. Who are the people in your life who are "up a tree"? Who are the least respectable, most lost among your relatives, neighbors, coworkers, and others?

7. How do you typically interact with those people?

8. How do you think Jesus would interact with them if he were in your shoes?

9. When you think about spending more time among lost, broken people, which (if any) of the following concerns do you struggle with?

☐ Being viewed as intolerant and therefore bad
☐ Exposing your own less-than-perfectly-Christlike personal life
☐ Exposing your children to people with sinful habits
☐ Appearing to condone sin
☐ Being judged by your Christian friends for associating with immoral people
☐ Adding more stress to your already stressful life

☐ Socializing with people with whom you have little in common (For example, their taste in entertainment, topics of conversation, or views on social issues are likely different from yours.)

☐ Giving up how and with whom you want to spend your time

10. Jesus faced some of the concerns listed in question 9. From the incident with Zacchaeus or other passages you're aware of, how did Jesus deal with each of the following concerns? What was his rationale?

☐ Appearing to condone sin
☐ Being judged for associating with immoral people
☐ Adding more stress to his already stressful life
☐ Socializing with people whose taste in entertainment, topics of conversation, or views on social issues were different from his

For other biblical responses to the concerns in question 9, see the passages in the For Deeper Study section that follows.

FOR DEEPER STUDY

Read Luke 5:27–32. With his limited time, Jesus made the "sick" a priority over the "healthy." To what extent do you think that would be a good model for you? How much time do you need to spend with the "healthy," and why? Why do you think Jesus didn't worry about appearing to condone sin when he dined with sinners?

How did Paul address the fear that our less-than-perfect lives make us invalid witnesses for Christ (2 Corinthians 4:5–12)?

We're less likely to lose our bearings among unbelievers if we are clear in our own minds about what is right and wrong. What behaviors are always right (Galatians 5:22–23)? What behaviors are always wrong (Galatians 5:19–21)? In disputable areas, how can we make up our minds (Romans 13:8–10;14:1–5; 1 Corinthians 6:12; 9:24–27)?

SHARING YOUR LIFE MISSION EVERY DAY   20 min.

11. Have you already held your outreach project? If not, finalize your plans now.

12. What has been the high point of this study for you? What have you gained?

SURRENDERING YOUR LIFE FOR GOD'S PLEASURE   15–30 min.

13. Are any group members going out in pairs to help launch a new group (session 5, question 10)? If so, let them be the focus of your prayer time. Invite them to share their biggest hope and their biggest fear.

   Then gather around them and pray for God to equip them fully for this ministry, to be powerfully present with them throughout, and to address their biggest fear. You might want to lay a hand on each one's shoulder as a gesture of support.

14. Close by thanking God for what he is doing in the lives of each group member.

STUDY NOTES

   The disciples often saw people like Zacchaeus as distractions rather than opportunities to extend love (Matthew 15:23, 32–33). Jesus regularly reminded them that people were the mission, not the distraction.

Chief tax collector (Luke 19:2). A high official who oversaw many tax collectors like Levi/Matthew (Luke 5:27–32). Tax collectors worked for the Roman invaders and made their profit by extorting money above what the Romans required. Their tactics were often cruel or violent. Zacchaeus became wealthy at his own people's expense.

I will pay back four times the amount (19:8). Paying back four times the amount was far more than what the Old Testament required (Leviticus 5:16; Numbers 5:7). Zacchaeus may have really gouged people, or he may have wanted to show his great repentance and devotion. Repentance should produce fruit (Luke 3:8; Matthew 12:33–37).

PRAYER AND PRAISE REPORT

Briefly share your prayer requests with the large group, making notations below. Then gather in smaller groups of two to four to pray for each other.

Date: _____

Prayer Requests

_____

_____

_____

_____

_____

_____

_____

_____

_____

_____

Praise Report

_____

_____

_____

_____

_____

_____

_____

_____

_____

_____

_____

Use this page to write out your prayers, your thoughts about your daily Bible reading, or your meditations on a verse from the passage you have already studied. Below are some suggested verses for meditation. The Bible Reading Plan is on page 89.

For Meditation: Luke 19:10

For Bible Reading:

- What is the gospel Paul wants to communicate?

- How does Paul want his readers to treat unbelievers?

DVD NOTES

If you are watching the accompanying *Sharing Christ Together* DVD, write down what you sense God saying to you through the speaker. (If you'd like to hear a sample of the DVD teaching segment, go to www.lifetogether.com/ExperiencingChristTogether.)

_____

_____

_____

_____

_____

_____

_____

_____

_____

_____

_____

_____

_____

_____

_____

_____

_____

_____

_____

_____

_____

_____

_____

_____

_____

What do we do on the first night of our group?

Like all fun things in life—have a party! A "get to know you" coffee, dinner, or dessert is a great way to launch a new study. You may want to review the LIFE TOGETHER Agreement (pages 76–77) and share the names of a few friends you can invite to join you. But most importantly, have fun before your study time begins.

Where do we find new members for our group?

This can be troubling, especially for new groups that have only a few people or for existing groups that lose a few people along the way. We encourage you to pray with your group and then brainstorm a list of people from work, church, your neighborhood, your children's school, family, the gym, and so forth. Then have each group member invite several of the people on his or her list. Another good strategy is to ask church leaders to make an announcement or allow a bulletin insert.

No matter how you find members, it's vital that you stay on the lookout for new people to join your group. All groups tend to go through healthy attrition—the result of moves, releasing new leaders, ministry opportunities, and so forth—and if the group gets too small, it could be at risk of shutting down. If you and your group stay open, you'll be amazed at the people God sends your way. The next person just might become a friend for life. You never know!

How long will this group meet?

It's totally up to the group—once you come to the end of this six-week study. Most groups meet weekly for at least the first six weeks, but every other week can work as well. We strongly recommend that the group meet for the first six months on a weekly basis if at all possible. This allows for continuity, and if people miss a meeting they aren't gone for a whole month.

At the end of this study, each group member may decide if he or she wants to continue on for another six-week study. Some groups launch relationships for years to come, and others are stepping-stones into another group experience. Either way, enjoy the journey.

Can we do this study on our own?

Absolutely! This may sound crazy but one of the best ways to do this study is not with a full house but with a few friends. You may choose to gather with one other couple who would enjoy going to the movies or having a quiet dinner and then walking through this study. Jesus will be with you even if there are only two of you (Matthew 18:20).

What if this group is not working for us?

You're not alone! This could be the result of a personality conflict, life stage difference, geographical distance, level of spiritual maturity, or any number of things. Relax. Pray for God's direction, and at the end of this six-week study, decide whether to continue with this group or find another. You don't buy the first car you look at or marry the first person you date, and the same goes with a group. Don't bail out before the six weeks are up—God might have something to teach you. Also, don't run from conflict or prejudge people before you have given them a chance. God is still working in you too!

Who is the leader?

Most groups have an official leader. But ideally, the group will mature and members will rotate the leadership of meetings. We have discovered that healthy groups rotate hosts/leaders and homes on a regular basis. This model ensures that all members grow, give their unique contribution, and develop their gifts. This study guide and the Holy Spirit can keep things on track even when you rotate leaders. Christ has promised to be in your midst as you gather. Ultimately, God is your leader each step of the way.

How do we handle the child care needs in our group?

Very carefully. Seriously, this can be a sensitive issue. We suggest that you empower the group to openly brainstorm solutions. You may try one option that works for a while and then adjust over time. Our favorite approach is for adults to meet in the living room or dining room, and to share the cost of a babysitter (or two) who can be with the kids in a different part of the house. In this way, parents don't have to be away from their children all evening when their children are too young to be left at home. A second option is to use one home for the kids and a second home (close by or a phone call away) for the adults. A third idea is to rotate the responsibility of providing a lesson or care for the children either in the same home or in another home nearby. This can be an incredible blessing for kids. Finally, the most common idea is to decide that you need to have a night to invest in your spiritual lives individually or as a couple, and to make your own arrangements for child care. No matter what decision the group makes, the best approach is to dialogue openly about both the problem and the solution.

To answer your further questions, we have created a website called www.lifetogether.com/ExperiencingChristTogether that can be your small group coach. Here are ten reasons to check out this website:

1. Top twenty questions every new leader asks
2. Common problems most new leaders face and ways to overcome them
3. Seven steps to building a healthy small group in six weeks
4. Free downloadable resources and leadership support
5. Additional leadership training material for every lesson in the EXPERIENCING CHRIST TOGETHER series
6. Ten stories from leaders who successfully completed this study
7. Free chat rooms and bulletin boards
8. Downloadable Health Assessments and Health Plans for individuals or groups
9. A chance to join a community of small group leaders by affinity, geography, or denominational affiliation
10. Best of all, a free newsletter with the best ideas from leaders around the world

LIFE TOGETHER AGREEMENT

OUR PURPOSE

To transform our spiritual lives by cultivating our spiritual health in a healthy small group community. In addition, we: _____

_____

_____.

OUR VALUES

Group Attendance	To give priority to the group meeting. We will call or email if we will be late or absent. (Completing the Small Group Calendar on page 78 will minimize this issue.)
Safe Environment	To help create a safe place where people can be heard and feel loved. (Please, no quick answers, snap judgments, or simple fixes.)
Respect Differences	To be gentle and gracious to people with different spiritual maturity, personal opinions, temperaments, or imperfections. We are all works in progress.
Confidentiality	To keep anything that is shared strictly confidential and within the group, and to avoid sharing improper information about those outside the group.
Encouragement for Growth	To be not just takers but givers of life. We want to spiritually multiply our life by serving others with our God-given gifts.
Welcome for Newcomers	To keep an open chair and share Jesus' dream of finding a shepherd for every sheep.
Shared Ownership	To remember that every member is a minister and to ensure that each attender will share a

| | small team role or responsibility over time. (See Team Roles on pages 79–81.) |
| **Rotating Hosts/Leaders and Homes** | To encourage different people to host the group in their homes, and to rotate the responsibility of facilitating each meeting. (See the Small Group Calendar on page 78.) |

OUR EXPECTATIONS

• Refreshments/mealtimes _____

• Child care _____

• When we will meet (day of week) _____

• Where we will meet (place) _____

• We will begin at (time)_____ and end at _____

• We will do our best to have some or all of us attend a worship service together. Our primary worship service time will be _____

• Date of this agreement _____

• Date we will review this agreement again _____

• Who (other than the leader) will review this agreement at the end of this study_____

SMALL GROUP CALENDAR

Planning and calendaring can help ensure the greatest participation at every meeting. At the end of each meeting, review this calendar. Be sure to include a regular rotation of host homes and leaders, and don't forget birthdays, socials, church events, holidays, and mission/ministry projects. Go to www.lifetogether.com for an electronic copy of this form and more than a hundred ideas for your group to do together.

Date	Lesson	Host Home	Dessert/Meal	Leader
Monday, January 15	1	Steve and Laura's	Joe	Bill

TEAM ROLES

The Bible makes clear that every member, not just the small group leader, is a minister in the body of Christ. In a healthy small group, every member takes on some small role or responsibility. It's more fun and effective if you team up on these roles.

Review the team roles and responsibilities below, and have each member volunteer for a role or participate on a team. If someone doesn't know where to serve or is holding back, have the group suggest a team or role. It's best to have one or two people on each team so you have each of the five purposes covered. Serving in even a small capacity will not only help your leader but also will make the group more fun for everyone. Don't hold back. Join a team!

The opportunities below are broken down by the five purposes and then by a *crawl* (beginning step), *walk* (intermediate step), or *run* (advanced step). Try to cover at least the crawl and walk roles, and select a role that matches your group, your gifts, and your maturity. If you can't find a good step or just want to see other ideas, go to www.lifetogether.com and see what other groups are choosing.

Team Roles	Team Player(s)

CONNECTING TEAM (Fellowship and Community Building)

Crawl: Host a social event or group activity in the first week or two.
_____
_____

Walk: Create a list of uncommitted members and then invite them to an open house or group social.
_____
_____

Run: Plan a twenty-four-hour retreat or weekend getaway for the group. Lead the Connecting time each week for the group.
_____
_____

GROWING TEAM (Discipleship and Spiritual Growth)

Crawl: Coordinate the spiritual partners for the _____
group. Facilitate a three- or four-person _____
discussion circle during the Bible study
portion of your meeting. Coordinate the
discussion circles.

Walk: Tabulate the Personal Health Assessments _____
and Health Plans in a summary to let _____
people know how you're doing as a group.
Encourage personal devotions through group discussions
and pairing up with spiritual (accountability) partners.

Run: Take the group on a prayer walk, or plan _____
a day of solitude, fasting, or personal retreat. _____

SERVING TEAM (Discovering Your God-Given Design for Ministry)

Crawl: Ensure that every member finds a _____
group role or team he or she enjoys. _____

Walk: Have every member take a gift test _____
(see www.lifetogether.com) and _____
determine your group's gifts. Plan a
ministry project together.

Run: Help each member decide on a _____
way to use his or her unique gifts _____
somewhere in the church.

SHARING TEAM (Sharing and Evangelism)

Crawl: Coordinate the group's Prayer and _____
Praise Report of friends and family _____
who don't know Christ.

Walk: Search for group mission opportunities _____
and plan a cross-cultural group activity. _____

Run: Take a small-group "vacation" to host a _____
six-week group in your neighborhood _____
or office. Then come back together
with your current group.

SURRENDERING TEAM (Surrendering Your Heart to Worship)

Crawl: Maintain the group's Prayer
and Praise Report or journal.   _____
                                                _____

Walk: Lead a brief time of worship each   _____
week (at the beginning or end of   _____
your meeting), either a cappella or
using a song from the DVD or the
LIFE TOGETHER Worship DVD/CD.

Run: Plan a unique time of worship through   _____
Communion, foot washing, night of   _____
prayer, or nature walking.

PERSONAL HEALTH ASSESSMENT

	Just Beginning	Getting Going	Well Developed

CONNECTING WITH GOD AND OTHERS

I am deepening my understanding of and friendship
with God in community with others. — 1 2 3 4 5

I am growing in my ability both to share and to
show my love to others. — 1 2 3 4 5

I am willing to share my real needs for prayer and
support from others. — 1 2 3 4 5

I am resolving conflict constructively and am
willing to forgive others. — 1 2 3 4 5

CONNECTING Total _____

GROWING IN YOUR SPIRITUAL JOURNEY

I have a growing relationship with God through regular
time in the Bible and in prayer (spiritual habits). — 1 2 3 4 5

I am experiencing more of the characteristics of
Jesus Christ (love, patience, gentleness, courage,
self-control, and so forth) in my life. — 1 2 3 4 5

I am avoiding addictive behaviors (food, television,
busyness, and the like) to meet my needs. — 1 2 3 4 5

I am spending time with a Christian friend (spiritual partner)
who celebrates and challenges my spiritual growth. — 1 2 3 4 5

GROWING Total _____

SERVING WITH YOUR GOD-GIVEN DESIGN

I have discovered and am further developing my
unique God-given design. — 1 2 3 4 5

I am regularly praying for God to show me
opportunities to serve him and others. — 1 2 3 4 5

I am serving in a regular (once a month or more)
ministry in the church or community. — 1 2 3 4 5

I am a team player in my small group by sharing
some group role or responsibility. — 1 2 3 4 5

SERVING Total _____

SHARING GOD'S LOVE IN EVERYDAY LIFE

I am cultivating relationships with non-Christians and praying
for God to give me natural opportunities to share his love. 1 2 3 4 5

I am praying and learning about where God can use me
and my group cross-culturally for missions. 1 2 3 4 5

I am investing my time in another person or group who
needs to know Christ. 1 2 3 4 5

I am regularly inviting unchurched or unconnected
friends to my church or small group. 1 2 3 4 5

SHARING Total _____

SURRENDERING YOUR LIFE TO GOD

I am experiencing more of the presence and
power of God in my everyday life. 1 2 3 4 5

I am faithfully attending services and my
small group to worship God. 1 2 3 4 5

I am seeking to please God by surrendering every
area of my life (health, decisions, finances,
relationships, future, and the like) to him. 1 2 3 4 5

I am accepting the things I cannot change and
becoming increasingly grateful for the life I've been given. 1 2 3 4 5

SURRENDERING Total _____

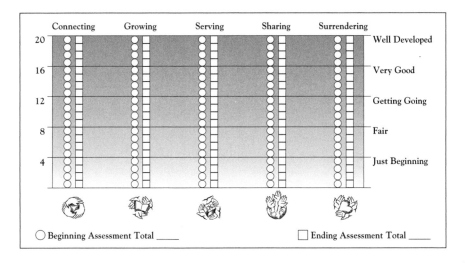

PERSONAL HEALTH PLAN

This worksheet could become your single most important feature in this study. On it you can record your personal priorities before the Father. It will help you live a healthy spiritual life, balancing all five of God's purposes.

PURPOSE	PLAN
CONNECT	WHO are you connecting with spiritually?
GROW	WHAT is your next step for growth?
DEVELOP	WHERE are you serving?
SHARE	WHEN are you shepherding another in Christ?
SURRENDER	HOW are you surrendering your heart?

Additional copies of the Personal Health Plan may be downloaded in a larger format at www.lifetogether.com/healthplan.

DATE	MY PROGRESS	PARTNER'S PROGRESS

SAMPLE PERSONAL HEALTH PLAN

This worksheet could become your single most important feature in this study. On it you can record your personal priorities before the Father. It will help you live a healthy spiritual life, balancing all five of God's purposes.

PURPOSE	PLAN
CONNECT	WHO are you connecting with spiritually? *Bill and I will meet weekly by email or phone.*
GROW	WHAT is your next step for growth? *Regular devotions or journaling my prayers 2x/week*
DEVELOP	WHERE are you serving? *Serving in Children's Ministry* *Go through GIFTS class*
SHARE	WHEN are you shepherding another in Christ? *Shepherding Bill at lunch or hosting a starter group in the fall*
SURRENDER	HOW are you surrendering your heart? *Help with our teenager* *New job situation*

DATE	MY PROGRESS	PARTNER'S PROGRESS
3/5	Talked during our group	Figured out our goals together
3/12	Missed our time together	Missed our time together
3/26	Met for coffee and review of my goals	Met for coffee
4/10	Emailed prayer requests	Bill sent me his prayer requests
3/5	Great start on personal journaling	Read Mark 1–6 in one sitting!
3/12	Traveled and not doing well this week	Journaled about Christ as Healer
3/26	Back on track	Busy and distracted; asked for prayer
3/1	Need to call Children's Pastor	
3/26	Group did a serving project together	Agreed to lead group worship
3/30	Regularly rotating leadership	Led group worship—great job!
3/5	Called Jim to see if he's open to joining our group	Wanted to invite somebody, but didn't
3/12	Preparing to start a group this fall	
3/30	Group prayed for me	Told friend something he's learning about Christ
3/5	Overwhelmed but encouraged	Scared to lead worship
3/15	Felt heard and more settled	Issue with wife
3/30	Read book on teens	Glad he took on his fear

JOURNALING 101

Henri Nouwen says effective and lasting ministry *for* God grows out of a quiet place alone *with* God. This is why journaling is so important.

The greatest adventure of our lives is found in the daily pursuit of knowing, growing in, serving, sharing, and worshiping Christ forever. This is the essence of a purposeful life: to see all five biblical purposes fully formed and balanced in our lives. Only then are we "complete in Christ" (Colossians 1:28, NASB).

David poured his heart out to God by writing psalms. The book of Psalms contains many of his honest conversations with God in written form, including expressions of every imaginable emotion on every aspect of his life. Like David, we encourage you to select a strategy to integrate God's Word and journaling into your devotional time. Use any of the following resources:

- Bible
- One-year Bible
- New Testament Bible Challenge Reading Plan (www.lifetogether.com/readingprograms)
- Devotional book
- Topical Bible study plan

Before or after you read a portion of God's Word, speak to God in honest reflection or response in the form of a written prayer. You may begin this time by simply finishing the sentence "Father . . . ," "Yesterday Lord . . . ,"or "Thank you, God, for. . . ." Share with him where you are at the present moment; express your hurts, disappointments, frustrations, blessings, victories, gratefulness. Whatever you do with your journal, make a plan that fits you so you'll have a positive experience. Consider sharing highlights of your progress and experiences with some or all of your group members, especially your spiritual partner(s). You may find they want to join and even encourage you in this journey. Most of all, enjoy the ride and cultivate a more authentic, growing walk with God.

BIBLE READING PLAN

36 Days in the Letters of Paul

In the other books in this series, the Bible Reading P lan typically leads you through one of the Gospels. In this book we invite you to spend thirty-six days in some of the letters the apostle Paul wrote to early believers. As you read, look for answers to these questions:

- What is the gospel Paul wants to communicate to the world?

- How does Paul want his readers to treat unbelievers? How will that behavior serve the spreading of the gospel?

Find a quiet place, and have ready a notebook or journal in which you can write what you learn and what you want to say back to God. You may also use the Reflections pages at the end of each session of this study.

☐ Day 1	Galatians 1	☐ Day 19	Colossians 3
☐ Day 2	Galatians 2	☐ Day 20	Colossians 4
☐ Day 3	Galatians 3	☐ Day 21	Romans 1
☐ Day 4	Galatians 4	☐ Day 22	Romans 2
☐ Day 5	Galatians 5	☐ Day 23	Romans 3
☐ Day 6	Galatians 6	☐ Day 24	Romans 4
☐ Day 7	Ephesians 1	☐ Day 25	Romans 5
☐ Day 8	Ephesians 2	☐ Day 26	Romans 6
☐ Day 9	Ephesians 3	☐ Day 27	Romans 7
☐ Day 10	Ephesians 4	☐ Day 28	Romans 8
☐ Day 11	Ephesians 5	☐ Day 29	Romans 9
☐ Day 12	Ephesians 6	☐ Day 30	Romans 10
☐ Day 13	Philippians 1	☐ Day 31	Romans 11
☐ Day 14	Philippians 2	☐ Day 32	Romans 12
☐ Day 15	Philippians 3	☐ Day 33	Romans 13
☐ Day 16	Philippians 4	☐ Day 34	Romans 14
☐ Day 17	Colossians 1	☐ Day 35	Romans 15
☐ Day 18	Colossians 2	☐ Day 36	Romans 16

LEADING FOR THE FIRST TIME

- **Sweaty palms are a healthy sign.** The Bible says God is gracious to the humble. Remember who is in control; the time to worry is when you're not worried. Those who are soft in heart (and sweaty-palmed) are those whom God is sure to speak through.

- **Seek support.** Ask your leader, coleader, or close friend to pray for you and prepare with you before the session. Walking through the study will help you anticipate potentially difficult questions and discussion topics.

- **Bring your uniqueness to the study.** Lean into who you are and how God wants you to uniquely lead the study.

- **Prepare. Prepare. Prepare.** Go through the session several times. If you are using the DVD, listen to the teaching segment and Leadership Lifter. Go to www.lifetogether.com and download pertinent files. Consider writing in a journal or fasting for a day to prepare yourself for what God wants to do.

- **Don't wait until the last minute to prepare.**

- **Ask for feedback so you can grow.** Perhaps in an email or on cards handed out at the study, have everyone write down three things you did well and one thing you could improve on. Don't get defensive, but show an openness to learn and grow.

- **Use online resources.** Go to www.lifetogether.com and listen to Brett Eastman share the weekly Leadership Lifter and download any additional notes or ideas for your session. You may also want to subscribe to the DOING LIFE TOGETHER Newsletter and LLT Newsletter. Both can be obtained for free by signing up at www.lifetogether.com/subscribe.

- **Prayerfully consider launching a new group.** This doesn't need to happen overnight, but God's heart is for this to happen over time. Not all

Christians are called to be leaders or teachers, but we are all called to be "shepherds" of a few someday.

- **Share with your group what God is doing in your heart.** God is searching for those whose hearts are fully his. Share your trials and victories. We promise that people will relate.

- **Prayerfully consider whom you would like to pass the baton to next week.** It's only fair. God is ready for the next member of your group to go on the faith journey you just traveled. Make it fun, and expect God to do the rest.

HOSTING AN OPEN HOUSE

If you're starting a new group, try planning an "open house" before your first formal group meeting. Even if you only have two to four core members, it's a great way to break the ice and to consider prayerfully who else might be open to join you over the next few weeks. You can also use this kick-off meeting to hand out study guides, spend some time getting to know each other, discuss each person's expectations for the group, and briefly pray for each other.

A simple meal or good desserts always make a kick-off meeting more fun. After people introduce themselves and share how they ended up being at the meeting (you can play a game to see who has the wildest story!), have everyone respond to a few icebreaker questions: "What is your favorite family vacation?" or "What is one thing you love about your church/our community?" or "What are three things about your life growing up that most people here don't know?" See www.lifetogether.com for more icebreaker ideas.

Next, ask everyone to tell what he or she hopes to get out of the study. You might want to review the LIFE TOGETHER Agreement (pages 76–77) and talk about each person's expectations and priorities.

Finally, set an open chair (maybe two) in the center of your group and explain that it represents someone who would enjoy or benefit from this group but who isn't here yet. Ask people to pray about whom they could invite to join the group over the next few weeks. Hand out postcards (see www.lifetogether.com for examples) and have everyone write an invitation or two. Don't worry about ending up with too many people—you can always have one discussion circle in the living room and another in the dining room after you watch the lesson. Each group could then report prayer requests and progress at the end of the session.

You can skip this kick-off meeting if your time is limited, but you'll experience a huge benefit if you take the time to connect with each other in this way.

EXPERIENCING CHRIST TOGETHER IN A SUNDAY SCHOOL SETTING

Sunday school is one of the best places to begin building community in your church, and the EXPERIENCING CHRIST TOGETHER DVDs and study guides work in concert to help your Sunday school leadership team do it easily and effectively.

Each study guide of the LIFE TOGETHER curriculum includes a companion DVD with today's top Christian leaders speaking to the passage of Scripture under discussion. Here is one way to use the DVD in a Sunday school class:

- Moderator introduction: welcome the class, and read the Scripture passage for the session
- DVD teaching segment: ten to fifteen minutes
- Small group discussion: divide into small groups of eight to twelve and, using the questions from the curriculum, discuss how the passage applies to each person in the class

So often Sunday school consists of the star teacher with little involvement from others. To use the EXPERIENCING CHRIST TOGETHER DVDs effectively means recruiting a host of people to participate in the Sunday school program. We recommend four teams:

Moderators. These are the facilitators or leaders of the class. Their role is to transition the class through each step in the time together. For example, the moderator will welcome the class and open with prayer. In addition, he or she will introduce the DVD segment by reading the Scripture passage for the session. We recommend that you recruit several moderaters. That allows you to rotate the moderators each week. Doing so takes the pressure off people to commit to every week of the class—and it offers more people opportunity for upfront leadership. One church recruited three sets of moderators (a total of six) because the Sunday school leaders wanted to use the curriculum for twelve weeks. They knew that out of twelve weeks, one set of moderators would, likely, burn out; it's difficult for anyone to provide leadership for twelve straight weeks.

Discussion Guides. These are people who lead the follow-up discussion after the DVD teaching segment. If, for example, your Sunday school runs for an hour, you may want to plan on fifteen to twenty minutes for the DVD teaching segment and an additional twenty to thirty minutes in small group discussion afterward. One church recruited many of its seniors to lead the discussion groups. Some of them had felt excluded from ministry, and the role of discussion guide opened the door for them to serve.

Each discussion guide needs only to read through the passage and the questions in each study guide for preparation. After the DVD teaching segment, the moderator of the class asks the discussion guides to stand up. Then, people circle their chairs around each discussion guide. It's an easy way to create small groups each week. You may need to help some groups find more people or other groups to divide once more, if they end up too large. One church asked some of the discussion guides to move their groups into different rooms, because the seniors had a hard time hearing.

Hospitality Coordinators. These are those who oversee the food and drink for the class. Some classes may not provide this, but for those who do, it's important that multiple people join the team, so one or two people don't burn out over the course of the class.

Technical Coordinators. There's nothing worse than a DVD player that doesn't seem to work. Recruit at least one person to oversee making sure the DVD works each week. It's best, though, to recruit two or three people, in order to rotate them throughout the Sunday school series. It's important that the technical team has made sure the DVD player works *before* the class begins.

One church decided to gather all the adult Sunday school classes together for a twelve-week series using the LIFE TOGETHER DVD and study guides. What happened was amazing—instead of Sunday school starting off with 140 people and ending up with half that many at the end of the fall, attendance stayed high the entire time. Instead of one Sunday school class being led by one or two teachers, more than thirty-five people were involved in some kind of leadership—as moderators, discussion guides, hospitality (food) coordinators, or technical coordinators. The fifteen-minute time at the beginning of Sunday school for coffee and snacks (fruit, coffee cake, etc.) proved just as valuable as the content portion!

The fall program gave the church a new vision for how Sunday school can support the larger issue of spiritual formation and life change. For more ideas and practical tools to strengthen your small group ministry, go to www.lifetogethertoday.com.

INTRODUCTION

By the end of this six-week study, our hope is that each member of your group will be motivated to reproduce Christ's life in one or more other people. Your group members have Christ's life within them because of their faith in him; they simply need to develop the motivation and habit of passing that life on to others. Even new believers have something to offer an unbeliever or another new believer.

Some group members will be drawn to lead another group, perhaps through the first study in this series, *Beginning in Christ Together*. They might take a six-week break from your group to do this, and then return to your group when they've raised up a new leader. Session 5 of this study explains more about that idea. Others will be motivated to plan a group outreach event. Sessions 2 and 4 contain ideas for that. Some will focus on unbelievers they already know through their daily lives. Some will want to get involved cross-culturally. Your job as leader is to help individuals identify their own passion for outreach and to encourage teams of two (or the whole group together) to take action.

The Bible studies in this guide focus on the development of group members' hearts. The goal is to acquire Jesus' compassion and commitment toward lost people. When people's deepest convictions and values are formed, those will motivate people for the long term.

SESSION ONE:
THE FATHER'S HEART

As a leader, your most important job is to create an atmosphere where people are willing to talk honestly about what Christ's words and actions have to do with them. Especially if your group is new, be available before people arrive so you can greet them at the door. People are naturally nervous at a new group, so a hug or handshake can help put them at ease.

Consider starting this first meeting half an hour early to give people time to socialize without shortchanging your study time. For example, you can have social time from 7:00 to 7:30, and by 7:40 you'll gather the group with a prayer. Even if only a few people are seated in the living room by 7:40, ask them to join you in praying for those who are coming and for God to be present among you as you meet. Others will notice you praying and will sit down.

You may ask a few people to come early to help set up, pray, and introduce newcomers to others. Even if everyone is new, they don't know that yet and may be shy when they arrive. You might give people roles like setting up nametags or handing out drinks. This could be a great way to spot a coleader.

Question 1. This first question enables members to get to know each other's situations and start thinking about the topic at hand. You should be the first to answer this question while others are thinking about how to respond. Set an example of a brief answer. Be sure to give everyone a chance to respond to this question. Your discussion will be more relaxed and genuine if you don't go around the circle in order.

Introduction to the Series. Take a moment after question 1 to orient the group to one principle that undergirds this series: *A healthy small group balances the purposes of the church.* Most small groups emphasize Bible study, fellowship, and prayer. But God has called us to reach out to others as well. He wants us to *do* what Jesus teaches, not just *learn about* it. You may spend less time in this series studying the Bible than some group members are used to. That's because you'll spend more time doing things the Bible says believers should do.

However, those who like more Bible study can find plenty of it in this series. At the end of each session, For Deeper Study provides more passages you can study on the same topic. If your group likes to do deeper Bible study, consider having members answer next week's Growing section questions ahead of time as homework. They can even study next week's For Deeper Study passages for homework too. Then, during the Growing portion of your meeting, you can share the high points of what you've learned.

If the five biblical purposes are new to your group, be sure to review them together on pages 8–10 of the Read Me First section.

Question 2. An agreement helps you clarify your group's priorities and cast new vision for what the group can be. Members can imagine what your group could be like if they lived these values. So turn to pages 76–77 and choose one value that you want to emphasize in this study. We've suggested an option that fits with this study's focus on outreach.

Question 3. Have someone read the Bible passage aloud. It's a good idea to ask someone ahead of time, because not everyone is comfortable reading aloud in public. When the passage has been read, ask question 3. *It is not necessary that everyone answer every question in the Bible study.* In fact, a group can become boring if you simply go around the circle and give answers. Your goal is to create a discussion—which means that perhaps only a few people respond to each question and an engaging dialogue gets going.

Jesus told the three stories in Luke 15 in response to a specific situation. The respectable and devout religious leaders of his day thought it was ungodly for him to spend his time with immoral people. Some group members may face the same kind of criticism. What will other Christians think if you spend time with unbelievers who are living with their girlfriend, who drink, or whose lives are a mess? If this is something your group members face, you can call attention to the fact that Jesus faced the same thing and responded by explaining the Father's heart toward people with messy lives.

Question 5. God deeply loves those who serve him faithfully, but he is passionate about pursuing and restoring those who don't. He views them as lost beloved ones. They are a high priority for him. While God does hate sin, he has compassion toward those who are trapped in slavery to sinful habits.

Question 8. Use the Study Notes to emphasize how outrageous the father's compassion is. He leaves the door open to his younger son, rather than rejecting him forever. He never gives up watching for the son (verse 20). He runs when the son returns, even though running is considered demeaning for a Middle Eastern man. He lavishes his son with welcome. He's even tender to his older son.

Question 11. Compassion doesn't come naturally. Culture trains us to respect a certain kind of person and look down on other kinds. Our hearts need to be deliberately renovated in order to see others as God does.

Questions 12 and 13. We've offered several options for personal time with God. Every believer should have a plan for personal time with God. Walk the group through these options.

Instead of reading Paul's letters, For Deeper Study is another option for those who prefer topical Bible study. If your group is accustomed to doing Bible study homework before each meeting, this is a great choice.

For those who have done a lot of Bible study, we encourage the meditation option. Living with one short passage each week can help them move biblical truth from their heads into their hearts and actions.

It's perfectly fine if one person chooses one option and another chooses another. One principle of life together is to champion each other's dreams and goals.

Question 14. For those who haven't done a LIFE TOGETHER study before, spiritual partners will be a new idea. We highly encourage you to try pairs or triplets for six weeks. It's so hard to sustain a spiritual practice like prayer or consistent Bible reading with no support. A friend makes a huge difference. Partners can check in with each other weekly either at the beginning of your group meetings or outside the meeting.

Question 16. Never pressure a person to pray aloud. That's a sure way to scare someone away from your group. So instead of praying in a circle (which makes it obvious when someone stays silent), allow open time when anyone can pray who wishes to. Have someone write down everyone's prayer requests on the Prayer and Praise Report (page 22). If your time is short, consider having people share requests and pray with just one or two other people.

SESSION TWO: CHRIST IN FLESH AND BLOOD

Question 1. If you prefer (and especially if there are many newcomers), question 1 will always be a lighter icebreaker for the whole group. We encourage you, though, to let partners check in at least every other week so that those relationships grow solid. Please don't miss this opportunity to take your people deeper. Remember that the goal here is "transforming lives through community," and one-on-one time has an enormous return on time spent. In a week or two, you might want to ask the group how their partnerships are going. This will encourage those who are struggling to connect or accomplish their goals.

If newcomers have joined you, take a few minutes before the Growing section to let all members introduce themselves. If you did question 1 rather than question 2, you could even let members tell one thing they've liked about the group so far, and let the newcomers tell who invited them. The first visit to a new group is scary, so be sure to minimize the inside jokes. Introduce newcomers to some highly relational people when they arrive and partner them with great spiritual partners to welcome them to their first meeting.

Question 3. Christ is the "Word"—direct the group to the study note about that. Christ is fully God and yet "with" God. That is, God the Son is distinct from God the Father, but along with the Holy Spirit they are the one God, three persons in one being. Everything was made through Christ. He is the source of life. For this study, the point of understanding these exalted things about Christ is to grasp how astounding it is that he took on human flesh to live among us humans. The more we're grateful for that, the more we'll be willing to live among the lost rather than isolating ourselves in a Christians-only community.

Question 4. He came to give light to those in darkness, to help them be reborn as God's intimate children, to reveal God's glory, to offer grace and truth. That's our mission too.

Question 5. He who was unlimited took on limits when he was born in a human body. He accepted pain, hunger, hatred, and everything else human except sin. On the cross he even bore our sin and suffered total separation from his Father.

Question 6. This is a profound theological question. Briefly, only God could carry the sin of the whole world, but only a human could represent the human race. Also, God wanted to show that he was willing to go through everything we go through. And he wanted to show that it was possible to live a human life without sinning. Finally, he wanted to show a few witnesses his glory, grace, and truth up close, in the flesh.

Question 7. Unbelievers are drawn to Christ when we treat them better than they treat us or each other. Unbelievers even take notice when we Christians treat each other with more love than they are used to seeing.

Question 8. Superior arguments alone don't convince most unbelievers. They need to see that following Christ actually makes a different kind of human being, one who loves as God loves. They need to see Christ in the flesh, in us. If they meet one individual who loves like that, they can assume that person is a fluke. If they meet a group of people who all routinely love sacrificially, they are forced to conclude that there really must be a God who loves, who changes people, and who provides for their deepest needs.

Question 11. It's important for the group to understand that they don't have to make room for new people in their busy lives in order to share their faith. At least a few people are already in their lives. Give everyone a minute to write down names, then share those names. Have someone compile a group list of at least ten people whom you'll pray for throughout this study.

Question 12. Set an example by telling which habit you are taking on. And be sure to follow through!

Question 13. As leader, you are in the people development business. Your job is to help group members grow into disciples and ministers over time. In order to discover and develop their unique gifts, they need opportunities to take on responsibilities in the group. But don't be shocked if they don't volunteer to take on the job of planning an outreach event. Most people would rather stay in the safety of the group than take action outside.

However, you probably know which one or two people are most gifted to plan a party or other outreach. You may need to go up to them during social time after the meeting and ask them to take on this job. Your personal invitation, and affirmation of their abilities, will make a huge difference to them. Another surefire approach is to ask the group which two people would be perfect for this task.

Afterward, don't let this drop. You'll need to check in with those outreach leaders to see how the plans are going. You'll need to offer help and cheerlead the rest of the group into participating.

SESSION THREE: SOWING SEEDS

In order to maximize your time together and honor the diversity of personality types, do your best to begin and end your meeting on schedule. You may even want to adjust your starting or stopping time. Don't hesitate to open in prayer even before everyone is seated. This isn't disrespectful of those who are still gathering—it respects those who are ready to begin, and the others won't be offended. An opening prayer can be as simple as, "Welcome, Lord! Help us! Now let's start."

If you've had trouble getting through all of the Bible study questions, consider breaking into smaller circles of four or five people for the Bible study portion of your meeting. Everyone will get more "airtime," and the people who tend to dominate the discussion will be balanced out. A circle of four doesn't need an experienced leader, and it's a great way to identify and train a coleader.

Question 1. Ask people to keep their responses to one minute. You should go first. This is practice for the kind of conversations you can have with unbelievers anytime. We often stick to safe topics like sports or work, but we need to have the courage to bring up subjects that really matter to people and that open the door for future conversations about God. The goal here is to have many conversations with someone over time about important things, so that when God eventually comes up, it comes across as natural, not as a sales pitch.

Questions 3 and 4. See "secrets of the kingdom of heaven" in the Study Notes. Jesus didn't try to unload the whole gospel on people at once, and we shouldn't either. He offered people a little at a time and waited to see how they responded before he offered more. Also, when he talked about salvation and God's kingdom, Jesus used stories and illustrations that his audience could understand. Stories didn't change his central message but they made it more appealing to people living in Palestine in the first century. He taught his disciples to share their faith the same way. Evangelism is like spreading seed on a hillside. Not all of it will take root and grow.

Question 6. The passage points to these obstacles: the evil one; life's inevitable hardships that make people doubt God if they expected him to make their lives easy; pressure from unbelievers to give up faith; distractions like wealth or just making a living.

Question 7. These are the kinds of emotions that can hinder us from persevering in sowing seeds when the results aren't immediate or dramatic. Set an example for your group by being honest about how you have felt after sharing your faith and getting a negative response.

Question 8. This is an important but difficult skill. Allow people time to practice. You may want to practice ahead of time and give them your best attempt as a model. These shouldn't be speeches; they should be short, the way normal conversations go. For instance, you might say, "All this pressure at work has really been getting to me. I've been praying about worry, and I think God is helping me deal with the stress without worrying so much about what will happen if things aren't perfect."

SESSION FOUR: WHO IS MY NEIGHBOR?

This session addresses outreach to people in other countries as well as outreach to people who live near you who come from a culture or lifestyle different from yours.

Question 4. As we often do, the legal expert wants rules: Whom am I expected to love, and whom can I overlook? Jesus focuses on our hearts: How can we expand our neighborliness to embrace those who are different from us?

Question 6. Jesus deliberately chose the ethnic group that would most shock his listeners. They were the traditional "bad guys." Is there a country, ethnic group, or type of person that your group of Christians traditionally treats as bad guys or unworthy of your attention? Those are exactly the people Jesus wants you to stop ignoring.

Question 8. We're busy. We can't pay attention to everyone and our culture trains us whom to ignore. It's natural to like people who are like us. Other groups may live in a separate section of town. They may speak a different language or have different customs. Be honest about the barriers for you, and talk about what you're willing to do to overcome them.

Question 12. You can fold this into your earlier plans for an outreach event. How can you include those from another culture? Or you can make this a separate outreach, perhaps through supporting a missionary.

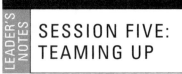

Question 3. Obviously, many things about this assignment were unique to that time. These disciples went to unfamiliar towns without money and with plans to find a stranger to stay with. Healing the sick was an important part of their ministry—it was evidence that their message about the kingdom was true. Still, many things about their assignment parallel ours: We too are lambs among wolves. We too are to prepare people to understand Jesus when he comes to them. We too face a plentiful field of people who don't know Christ and too few believers to reach them. The urgency today is the same as then.

Question 5. This is a chance for people to vent any discomfort they feel at work or in other settings where typically there are many unbelievers and few believers. The best way to deal with fear is to voice it among friends and pray about it.

Question 7. These disciples didn't have seminary training. They simply had spent months with Jesus, watching what he did and listening to what he said. Now they were ready to practice doing what he did. We too are qualified if we've been with Jesus and if we have the Holy Spirit inside us. It definitely helps if we've had a person to mentor us whom we can copy. But methods will vary from situation to situation. More important than methods is to have Jesus' character, to reflect his heart toward people. Loving and serving people cover most of the job. If we can do that, the words will come. Theological expertise is not necessary.

Question 9. Partners can encourage each other through failure. They can brainstorm how to deal with a situation. They can protect each other from temptation when spending time among people with immoral habits. Most of all, they can demonstrate how believers love one another. They can prove that love is normal among Christians. Jesus said outsiders would know his message was true when they saw Christians love each other (John 13:34–35; 17:22–23).

Question 10. This may seem like a shocking idea, but we've seen it work over and over. Your group won't end; you'll just take a break to do what you've been talking about: give away what you've been given. Are there even two people in your group who have the shepherd's heart to help another group get started? If so, talk to those people after your meeting. Their starter group could even be a group of believers. The idea is to practice the habit of giving away what God has given you. If you don't know whom to invite to a new group, ask your pastor.

One final thing in this session is to confirm the group's interest in continuing to another study in this series. Show them the next study guide and collect the money in advance, or pick up the books and have them pay you later.

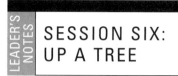

Whether your group is ending or continuing, it's important to celebrate where you have come together. If you choose not to discuss question 1 during your meeting, this would be a great question to discuss at a party. Be sure the spiritual partner time is honored.

Thank everyone for what they've contributed to the group. You might even give some thought ahead of time to something unique each person has contributed. You can say those things at the beginning of your meeting.

Question 2. Zacchaeus must have known his life wasn't working. We need to watch for the signs people give that they're at least partly aware that they need something more. They may not say it, but they do something that shows it.

Question 3. Jesus wanted to open the gates of the kingdom to a man who was ready for it, as well as illustrate for his disciples and the crowd that God loved the very lost people, not just the "good" people. Also, Jesus was so convinced that his Father loved and approved of him that he wasn't driven by a craving to be approved by people (John 5:20, 41–44; 13:3).

Question 4. A genuine encounter with Jesus produces some evidence of repentance, of a changed life. When leading people to Christ, we need to be careful not to give them the idea that faith is simply an intellectual exercise. We need to make it clear that part of being a Christian is letting Jesus point out areas of our lives where we need to change.

Question 6. Try to help every group member think of at least one person.

Question 9. Set an example by honestly sharing your own concerns. These struggles need to be on the table and dealt with. You may be able to help each other. For instance, it's legitimate to worry about your children if unbelievers are the only influence on them. But if you team up with another family, your kids will have you and the other family as models of what an abundant life is like. If you are genuinely loving one another, your kids will be smart enough to make good choices. In fact, they will be part of your witness to unbelievers.

Question 13. If people from your group are going out temporarily to serve another group, be sure to show them a tremendous demonstration of your support. Plan a time with special desserts to celebrate the end of this study and the action these members are about to take.

ABOUT THE AUTHORS

The authors' previous work as a team includes the DOING LIFE TOGETHER Bible study series, which won a Silver Medallion from the Evangelical Christian Publishers Association, as well as the DOING LIFE TOGETHER DVD series.

Brett Eastman has served as the champion of Small Groups and Leadership Development for both Willow Creek Community Church and Saddleback Valley Community Church. Brett is now the Founder and CEO of Lifetogether, a ministry whose mission is to "transform lives through community." Brett earned his Masters of Divinity degree from Talbot School of Theology and his Management Certificate from Kellogg School of Business at Northwestern University. **Dee Eastman** is the real hero in the family, who, after giving birth to Joshua and Breanna, gave birth to identical triplets—Meagan, Melody, and Michelle. They live in Las Flores, California.

Todd and Denise Wendorff serve at King's Harbor Church in Redondo Beach, California. Todd is a teaching pastor, handles leadership development, and pastors men. He is also coauthor of the Every Man Bible Study Series. Denise speaks to women at conferences, classes, and special events. She also serves women through personal discipleship. Previously, Todd was on the pastoral staff at Harvest Bible Chapel, Willow Creek Community Church, and Saddleback Valley Community Church. He holds a Th.M. from Talbot School of Theology. Todd and Denise live in Rolling Hills Estates, California with their three children, Brooke, Brittany, and Brandon.

Karen Lee-Thorp has written or cowritten more than fifty books and Bible studies, including *How to Ask Great Questions* and *Why Beauty Matters*. Her previous Silver Medallion winners are *The Story of Stories*, *LifeChange: Ephesians*, and *LifeChange: Revelation*. She was a senior editor at NavPress for many years and series editor for the LifeChange Bible study series. She is now a freelance writer, speaks at women's retreats, and trains small group leaders. She lives in Brea, California, with her husband, Greg Herr, and their daughters, Megan and Marissa.

SMALL GROUP ROSTER

Name	Address	Phone	Email Address	Team or Role	Church Ministry
Bill Jones	7 Alvalar Street L.F. 92665	766-2255	bjones@aol.com	socials	children's ministry

(Pass your book around your group at your first meeting to get everyone's name and contact information.)

Name	Address	Phone	Email Address	Team or Role	Church Ministry

Experiencing Christ Together:
Living with Purpose in Community
Brett & Dee Eastman; Todd & Denise Wendorff;
Karen Lee-Thorp

Experiencing Christ Together: Living with Purpose in Community is a series of six, six-week study guides that offers small groups a chance to explore Jesus' teaching on the five biblical purposes of the church. By closely examining Christ's life and teaching in the Gospels, the series helps group members walk in the steps of Christ's early followers. Jesus lived every moment following God's purposes for his life, and Experiencing Christ Together helps groups learn how they can do this too. The first book lays the foundation: who Christ is and what he has done for us. Each of the other five books in the series looks at how Jesus trained his followers to live one of the five biblical purposes (fellowship, disciple-ship, service, evangelism, and worship).

	Softcovers	DVD
Beginning in Christ Together	ISBN: 0-310-24986-4	ISBN: 0-310-26187-2
Connecting in Christ Together	ISBN: 0-310-24981-3	ISBN: 0-310-26189-9
Growing in Christ Together	ISBN: 0-310-24985-6	ISBN: 0-310-26192-9
Serving Like Christ Together	ISBN: 0-310-24984-8	ISBN: 0-310-26194-5
Sharing Christ Together	ISBN: 0-310-24983-X	ISBN: 0-310-26196-1
Surrendering to Christ Together	ISBN: 0-310-24982-1	ISBN: 0-310-26198-8

Pick up a copy today at your favorite bookstore!

ZONDERVAN™

GRAND RAPIDS, MICHIGAN 49530 USA

WWW.ZONDERVAN.COM

Doing Life Together series

Brett & Dee Eastman; Todd & Denise Wendorff;
Karen Lee-Thorp

Based on the five biblical purposes that form the bedrock of Saddleback Church, Doing Life Together will help your group discover what God created you for and how you can turn this dream into an everyday reality. Experience the transformation firsthand as you begin Connecting, Growing, Developing, Sharing, and Surrendering your life together for him.

"Doing Life Together is a groundbreaking study . . . [It's] the first small group curriculum built completely on the purpose-driven paradigm . . . The greatest reason I'm excited about [it] is that I've seen the dramatic changes it produces in the lives of those who study it."
—FROM THE FOREWORD BY RICK WARREN

Small Group Ministry Consultation

Building a healthy, vibrant, and growing small group ministry is challenging. That's why Brett Eastman and a team of certified coaches are offering small group ministry consultation. Join pastors and church leaders from around the country to discover new ways to launch and lead a healthy Purpose-Driven small group ministry in your church. To find out more information please call 1-800-467-1977.

	Softcover	
Beginning Life Together	ISBN: 0-310-24672-5	ISBN: 0-310-25004-8
Connecting with God's Family	ISBN: 0-310-24673-3	ISBN: 0-310-25005-6
Growing to Be Like Christ	ISBN: 0-310-24674-1	ISBN: 0-310-25006-4
Developing Your SHAPE to Serve Others	ISBN: 0-310-24675-X	ISBN: 0-310-25007-2
Sharing Your Life Mission Every Day	ISBN: 0-310-24676-8	ISBN: 0-310-25008-0
Surrendering Your Life for God's Pleasure	ISBN: 0-310-24677-6	ISBN: 0-310-25009-9
Curriculum Kit	ISBN: 0-310-25002-1	

ZONDERVAN™

GRAND RAPIDS, MICHIGAN 49530 USA

WWW.ZONDERVAN.COM

life**together**.com

Life Together Student Edition
Brett Eastman & Doug Fields

The Life Together series is the beginning of a relational journey, from being a member of a group to being a vital part of an unbelievable spiritual community. These books will help you think, talk, dig deep, care, heal, share . . . and have the time of your life! Life . . . together!

The Life Together Student Edition DVD Curriculum combines DVD teaching from well-known youth Bible teachers, as well as leadership training, with the Life Together Student Edition Small Group Series to give a new way to do small group study and ministry with basic training on how to live healthy and balanced lives-purpose driven lives.

Pick up a copy today at your favorite bookstore!

ZONDERVAN™

GRAND RAPIDS, MICHIGAN 49530 USA

WWW.ZONDERVAN.COM